Pa

MW01493742

How to patent an idea.

Patent Your Idea and Sell Your Idea.

UK and USA patent information.

By

Lewis Durton

Table of Contents

General Introduction

Everybody will want to benefit fully from their inventions and exclude and prevent others from using them with their authorisation. However, man by nature is selfish and greedy. The innate greed and envy in man pushes him to seek for gain and even to the extent of appropriating what belongs to another person if unrestrained. This inborn selfishness, envy and greed are also the reasons why one will want to exclude others from using or benefiting from their creation, ideas and invention. Every inventor would not want others to use their ideas. The civilised society uses patent rights to checkmate these aspects of man. A patent excludes others from using another person's invention or idea but only for a limited time. In other words, this exclusive right is not eternal. Others can take advantage of an invention after the expiration of the patent rights.

Patent rights also have limitations and exceptions. Not everything can be patented. It also does not cover improvements on the original idea or invention unless such improvement involves an inventive step or is nonobvious to people with experience and knowledge in the area. An invention here can refer to a solution to a particular technological problem. It can also mean a process or a product. Put differently, patents are types of intellectual property. However, each sovereign state has its unique patent legislation even though there are similarities among the patent rules of various countries. The major differences in the patent legislation of various countries lie in the requirements for obtaining the exclusive rights, the procedure of obtaining them and their scope.

This book is meant to serve as a practical guide on how you can patent your idea or invention to prevent others from using it. It also provides insights into how you can make some money from your patented idea. Patent is a commonly used term but some people confuse it with other similar terms such as copyright, servicemarks and trademarks. To ensure a proper understanding of the term, this book also takes a look at the meaning of patent and its legal implications.

"Patent Your Idea and Sell Your Idea" is divided into four different sections with each section containing at least a chapter. The first section examines the meaning of the terms. The second and third sections take a look at the practice of patenting in the US and the UK respectively. The last section is a guide on how you can sell your idea for profit. You will also find answers to many frequently asked questions about patents in this book. Helpful resources and websites are also provided.

Important note: at the time of printing, all the websites and contact details in this book are correct. As the internet changes rapidly, some sites might no longer be live or contact details might be wrong, when you read this book. This is, of course, out of our control.

Section 1: An Insight into the Meaning of Patent

A patent is a type of intellectual property right. It is similar to copyrights, servicemarks and trademarks. But it is a unique type of right, which should not be confused with other types of rights. Patents are of different kinds. In this section of the book, you will learn the meaning of a patent, its types, how it differs from other intellectual property rights and why it is important for you to have it.

Chapter One: Understanding What A Patent Is All About

Many people's ideas are ripped off because of their failure to protect and secure them with a patent. They don't know what a patent is all about, let alone knowing the process and requirements of obtaining it. Indeed, you will not think of applying for a patent if you don't know what it is all about, its types, how it differs from other kinds of intellectual properties and its benefits. Applying for it will not make any sense to you. This is why I deem it right to explain what a patent is all about from this early stage. With a proper understanding of what it is, you will appreciate why you should patent your ideas. Read on to learn more about this type of intellectual right.

What Is A Patent?

A patent refers to the rights given to an inventor or an assignee by a country to exclude others from using, making, exporting and implementing an invention within a specified period of time. In exchange, the patentee discloses the invention to the public. The right ensures that nobody uses the invention for commercial purposes when it is disclosed to the public, except with an express permission of the owner of the invention. A look at the etymology of the word patent will help you to understand it more. The word patent is derived from the Latin word "patere" which means to disclose, lay open, to expose, to make accessible etc. (to make a thing available for the public assessment).

The term and its usage have evolved overtime. Before the modern usage, patent, called "letters patent", referred to exclusive rights enshrined in an open document issued by a monarch or a government to a person or an entity. The US government, before this era, normally granted individuals with the sole rights over certain lands in a document called land patents. In the modern times, the term is used to designate exclusive rights given to inventors of new things, ideas, processes, designs, plants and others. What can be patented is stipulated in the constitutions of different countries. In other words, what is patentable in one country may not be patentable in another country. This explains why we have different kinds of patents such as design, utility, plant, medical and other types of patents as we shall see later in this book.

The patent rights are issued in order to encourage innovation, productivity and inventiveness in the society. However, before any inventor is issued with a patent, the invention must satisfy certain criteria contained in the patent law of the jurisdiction of the inventor. Most jurisdictions issue patents to only "non-obvious and novel" ideas, products, processes and methods. An invention is considered non-obvious if an expert in the area sees it as an unforeseen and extraordinary occurrence or discovery. A new or novel invention is one that is unique either in all its aspects or one or more of its aspects from existing inventions.

As we shall see later, not all novel inventions are patentable. For example, new ideas or suggestions can only be patented if the inventor is able to discover concrete ways of executing or actualising them. Under US law, patents are not issued to harmful inventions like unsafe drugs or invention that have no legal purpose. Similarly, newly discovered naturally occurring substances and natural laws are not protected by patents. The same thing applies to abstract principles, mathematical formulas, calculation methods and fundamental truths. However, you can apply for a patent if you invent a process or a thing that makes use of these substances, formulas or methods.

You can see that it is not enough to invent or discover a process, an idea or a thing for one to apply for a patent. It has to be novel, not naturally occurring elements or law and non-obvious. Patent rights do not cover just one type of thing. Utilities, medical devices, designs, computers, software, musical instruments, jewellery, drugs, chemical formulas and processes and genetically engineered plants, animals and plants can be covered by patents in different jurisdictions, including the US. This is why there are different kinds of patents.

Types of Patent

As I mentioned above, a lot of things ranging from concrete items to processes and chemical formulas can be patented. Patentable items, ideas and processes are grouped into three main types, namely, utility, design and plant utilities. Here, I am going to explain each of them one after the other.

Utility Patent

Patent for invention, better known as utility patent, is a type of patent right granted to inventors of machines, processes, products, pharmaceutical and medical equipment, chemical composition, medicines, tools, and other concrete items. However, it does not cover only concrete articles and items. It can cover certain immaterial realities. For example, this type of patent right can cover investment strategies, computer software and apps and similar nontangible realities. Improvements on existing inventions are also protected with a utility patent. Given that a lot of things come under this patent, it is the most common type of patent. It is in most cases used as a synonymous term with patent.

Utility patents are classified into five categories, which include the following:

1. A composition of matter
2. Improvement on existing invention, idea or strategy
3. A process
4. A manufacture
5. A machine

There are some inventions that can be classified into more than a group. For example, computer software, when considered together with the hardware through which it functions, can be seen as a computer (a device that accepts data and processes it to give the required result/output). However, it is also taken to be a process, when viewed as a programmes installed in a computer for processing of commands and specific tasks. Whether an invention falls into one category or multiple categories, it can only be protected with one utility patent. Below are various kinds of inventions and creative works that can be protected with this type of patent:

- Electronic circuits
- Computer hardware
- Processes/procedures
- Computer software, programmes and apps
- Computer hardware and peripherals
- New chemical formulas
- Biological inventions
- Electrical inventions
- Magic tricks
- Food inventions
- Machines
- Housewares

- Pharmaceutical/medical equipment including drugs

Once you are issued with this type of patent, you have the exclusive rights over the invention for which it is issued. No other person can use, sell, export or import it without your permission otherwise, you can file for patent infringement and seek for compensation for an illegal utilisation of your product. I shall talk about the duration of patent in another chapter below, but suffice it to mention that it differs from one jurisdiction to another. In the US for example, a utility patent gives an inventor an exclusive right over the inventions covered for a period of 20 years starting from the date the patent application is lodged.

Note that it is costlier to secure this type of patent than to acquire a design patent. This is because of the certain charges involved such as maintenance fees. Besides, being more expensive, it also takes a longer time for this type of patent to be issued. This also depends on your country. Overall, it may take about two to three years to get a patent for your invention starting from the date the application is lodged. On the positive aspect, its scope and coverage are broader.

To be issued with a utility patent, the applicant is required to meet certain conditions different from the general requirements mentioned above. In the first instance, your invention should be operable or usable. No matter how wonderful, amazing and captivating your invention might be, if it cannot be used, you will not receive any patent whether your invention is of practical relevance or has some benefits. Another condition which an invention must satisfy before a utility patent is issued to an inventor is that it must be of practical use. Practical use here is different from operability even though they are tightly connected. Practicability refers to the real-world use. You may easily establish this type of patent for different kinds of inventions except chemical compounds. This is because their practical function is sometimes determined after they have been developed. Thirdly, an invention has to be beneficial. Certain aspects of this requirement are no longer obtainable. For example, an immoral or deceptive invention under this requirement was initially not covered with a patent. Typical examples of inventions that are traditionally considered immoral and deceptive are gambling machines, sex toys and others. But today, such restrictions are no longer obtainable.

NB! A product can be protected by both a utility patent and a design patent, which secure the visual elements of the products. Also bear in mind that the exclusive right obtained under utility patent covers the structure as well as the manner in which the invention functions. In others, if another person makes a product that functions in the same manner with a patented product but has different structure, the individual may be found guilty of patent infringement.

The process of the application of utility patent, just as it is the case with other types of patents, differs from country to country. So, it will be good to discuss the process in the sections for patents in the UK and US.

Design Patent

As implicit from the name, a design patent is a type of patent issued to creators of unique visual elements of manufactured products. Visual elements or attributes include specific structural configuration and unique surface ornamentation as well as both. In other words, it is issued to protect product designs or appearance. The design here should not be confused with the functional aspect of a product. It is limited only to aesthetic or ornamental purposes. If the function of a product is embedded in the design, the right type of patent to cover such product may be a utility patent and design patent. For a product to be issued with a design patent, its design should be new, original and aesthetically valuable and important. However, the design does not exist in itself, in isolation or in a vacuum. It should inhere or bw applied to a manufactured product.

Consequently, it is important that you be able to differentiate between design and utility patents. There seems to be no difference between the two since it is almost impossible to have a design without a product. But they are not the same, as design only protects the aesthetic elements of a product and not its mechanical structure and functional aspects. This is why it is possible for a product to have both a design and utility patent, as I have already mentioned above.

A design patent gives a company or inventor leverage or a stronger competitive advantage over a competitor. If you come up with a design that is more attractive and captivating than those of your competitor, definitely, you are going to make more sales than they will do because consumers are also moved by the visual appeal of a product that they want to purchase. Taking the above into consideration, if you have a design patent, you should ensure nobody violates your rights. A design patent, like any other type of patent, is enforceable in a law court. You can sue any person that uses or sells your design without your permission for patent infringement. Apple has taken Samsung to court for the infringement of their iPhone design patents and they won the case. They were reportedly compensated by Samsung with a large sum of over $90 million (£64.4 million).

There is the tendency for some people to disregard this type of patent because it is not expensive and because it is quite easy to obtain. Many inventors go for utility patent rights and overlook the importance of protecting the design of their inventions. But shrewd inventors and big companies such as automakers (like Mercedes), shoemaking companies (like Adidas), electronic and mobile device producers (like Apple) always secure the design patent rights. But the Apple court case with Samsung is eloquent proof that design patents are great assets. It helps you to make more sales, increasing your revenue. You can also make money from its infringement.

Generally speaking, the process of obtaining this type of patent is not as complicated and time-consuming as the process of obtaining a utility patent. They are not commonly sought for as the utility patent.

Consequently, they are more affordable or inexpensive than a utility patent. Another factor that makes this type of patent more affordable is that it does not attract any maintenance fee until it expires.

Just as with patents of inventions, the duration of a design patent depends on the jurisdiction that issues it. In the United States of America, for example, if you own a design patent, you have an exclusive right over the design for a period of 14 years, which begins from the date it is issued to you.

If you are seeking for design patent rights, it is of crucial importance that you understand what you are seeking for and what you are granted. Design patents always come with some limitations. You need to understand these limitations. For example, it does not secure an invention or an idea. I have also mentioned that it does not cover the structure or functional mechanism of a product. This is why it is regarded as a weaker kind of patent. However, when you lodge the application for a design patent, it is recommended that you secure each unique variation or each unique appearance of your invention rather than go for one aspect. You will get the most out of your design if you secure all unique aspects of your drawings.

Note that a design patent is not given arbitrarily. Before you are issued with a design patent, it has to be established beyond reasonable doubt that the appearance or presentation of your invention is unique and different from the general appearance or structure of similar products. For example, every knife comes with a sharp edge those functions as the blade and a handle. Constructing a knife with an edge and handle, for example, is not enough to grant you a design patent. Rather, a design patent will be given to you on the basis of the uniqueness of your knife. This is why in determining a design patent infringement, the judge is obliged to consider in its entirety, the drawing of the product or invention to see whether it is original or copied. It protects only what is contained in the drawing. In other words, it does not concern the interior aspects of an invention. Its main domain is the exterior of an invention, which is what appears on the drawing.

Plant Patent

Green revolution, which ended the old agricultural practices, brought a lot of changes and innovation in agricultural practices. Plants are no longer populated and grown only with the seeds, tubers, grafting, budding and other naturally accepted means. They can be discovered or asexually made in the lab or a controlled environment. It is also possible for plants to be genetically altered to produce a particular kinds of plant. These changes explain why patents are granted to plant breeders. A patent right granted to inventors of plants is what is referred to as plant patents (note that in the UK, there is a separate right for plant breeders). This type of patent encourages innovation and inventiveness in modern agriculture and plant development. People who work hard to develop plants should benefit from their effort and work.

The process and requirements for granting this type of patent differs from place to place. It may not be obtainable in some countries. But it is one of the kinds of patents issued in the US and some other countries. If you are planning to apply for it, you have to find out what the law governing such a patent in your country demands from applicants.

It is not a commonly sought for patent. Normally, it is granted to people that discover new, nonobvious, genetically modified and asexually produced plants. In asexual production of plants, seeds and tubers are not used to grow new plants. Plants produced through asexual productions or genetic mutations are normally unique and distinct from the original plants from which they are made. Some of the hybrid plants are asexually reproduced.

For a plant to be patented and patentable, it has to meet certain requirements. First, it must be asexually reproduced. An asexually produced plant is any plant that is not produced through the natural means of producing plants. This means that the inventor or any other person will be able to reproduce the plant following the same process used by the inventor.

A patentable plant should have the same genetic constitution with the original plant and it has to be produced through budding, grafting, bulbs, division and cutting. Some plants are not patentable like potatoes and other tubers, bacteria and plants that become unique as a result of environmental influence or the nature of soil they are grown in. A plant found in an uncultivated state or in the wild, even if it is not yet known, is not patentable. For a plant to be patented, it also has to be non-obvious.

Each jurisdiction may have other requirements for the granting of this type of patent. For example, in the US, before the USPTO provides a plant inventor with a patent, the person must provide a comprehensive botanical description of the plant detailing all the unique features of the plant and showing its uniqueness in a drawing. The application for a plant patent must be lodged within a year of releasing or selling it. The inventor is also expected not to publicise the invention in print for over a period of a year.

The inventor of a plant is not determined in plant patents, like inventors of design, products, processes, mechanism and the likes. In a plant patent, it is possible for two people to be the inventors of a plant. This is because the process of inventing a plant involves two steps. The first is the discovering of a unique plant and second is the reproduction of the plant asexually. One person may discover and asexually reproduce a patentable plant. But there are also instances where one person or more discovers a unique plant and another person or group of people reproduce it asexually. In these instances, the plant has more than one inventor. Thus, an inventor of plants includes any person that makes a remarkable contribution in discovering of or/and asexual reproduction of a new plant. Put differently, team work is acknowledged in a plant patent. So, all the members of a team that discover or asexually reproduce a plant are co-inventors. However, in a situation where an inventor hires a service for the asexual reproduction of the plant, it is taken as a work-for-hire and therefore the service provider has no credit over the invention. Thus, a person is not regarded as a co-inventor and should not benefit from the discovery except for their pay.

Having a plant patent does not stop you from having the other two types of patents discussed above. If you secure a plant patent it should last for a period of 20 years starting from the date you lodged in the application (as it is the case in the US). Depending on your invention, you can also seek for a utility and design patent for complete protection of your plant. For example, if you discover and reproduce a plant with a unique look or structure, you can apply for a patent to exclude others from copying, reproducing or using it. The same thing could be said of a patent of invention.

Note that an exclusive right over some plants, plant-reproduction processes and seeds can be secured with a utility patent. You should also bear in mind that like other kinds of patents, plant patents have some limitations. Sport or mutants resulting from a plant with a patent are not protected by the original patent because they are not considered as belonging to the inventors of the original plant. For an inventor to have rights of mutants or sports, he or she has to seek for a separate plant patent for them. Put differently, a plant patent only excludes other people from selling or reproducing the original plant.

Proving the Uniqueness of a Plant

As already mention above, plant patents are only granted for plants that are unique. You need to show that your plant is unique before you will be issued with a patent for plants. Having just one unique feature is enough to secure a plant patent for a plant on the basis of this feature insofar as other requirements are met. The best way to ascertain and prove the uniqueness of your plant is to carry out a patent search. From the search, you will be able to find out if there are already patented plants with the same features as yours.

Medical Patent

A medical patent is classified by some authors under the utility patent. But there are other authors that treat them differently. Here, I am going to examine it as a separate kind of patent because of the importance of medical/pharmaceutical equipment and items. A medical patent is a type of protection given to inventors of unique of items and equipment that are medically valuable or that are used to accomplish a medical procedure against market competition. Software, applications and machines used for medical facilities for the better management of patients and equipment used for various kinds of therapies and medical tests are also protected with medical patents. It also includes novel medical process. The medical patent rights give an inventor an exclusive right to sell, use and produce the patented item.

Medical patents are valuable and highly cherished by biotech companies as they have them to gain fully from their invention within a stipulated number of years. Before a medical patent elapses, the inventor would have gained ground in the market and made a lot of profits from their invention. However, this may not secure the interest of consumers, especially low-earning patients because the patentees have a monopoly of the market and sell at a price that pleases them. This explains why newly patented medications, pharmaceutical and medical equipment are very expensive.

It is possible for multiple companies to benefit from a patented medical item even though the patent belongs to a company. This situation occurs if a company that has the license to use a patented item is different from the company that owns the patent.

Medical patents, like other types of patents, are enforceable in court. If you feel that your patent right is being violated by another company, you can go to court to seek for compensation and to stop the company from the illegal use, selling or production of your product. Medical patent infringement cases are a big problem to investors in the company that violates another company's medical patent. This is because apart from the compensation that they may be asked to pay, the court may also forbid them from further production.

Medical patents, also called biotechnology patents, are hotly debated today. The proponents believe that allowing it will engender progress in medical and scientific research because those that painstakingly come up with useful invention will make a fortune from it which will be a huge inducement to them. However, the opponents tagged it immoral or ethically unsound because of the high prices at which the inventors of these medical equipment, items, processes and machines tend to sell them at. According to this group of people, patented medicines and medical supplies are normally not within the financial means of low-income earners, especially people in the developing countries.

The above does not exhaust the available types of patent. Some laws of some countries may have more. But I limit myself to the three classifications used by the US patent laws as they are widely accepted.

Why You Should Patent Your Ideas

Undoubtedly, there are a lot of inventors and manufacturers of products who did not get the full benefits of their efforts or even lost completely to other people because they did not seek for patent protection. Some of them didn't apply because they were ignorant of how to obtain an exclusive right of one's invention while some didn't know that another could rip them of their effort by being the first to patent their inventions.

Thus, I am going to explain the various ways in which patenting your ideas would be of benefit to you. Here are some of the benefits of patent rights.

In the first instance, protecting your invention with patent right gives you peace of mind arising from the knowledge that you have the support of the law against any unauthorised use, production or sale of your invention, design, plant, process and the likes. Patenting your idea is a pure justification of your ownership over the idea. It makes you the real owner of the idea and gives you the right to seek for compensation and redress if another infringes on it.

Patenting your idea will be advantageous to you if you want another country to hold the license of your product. Having a patent right over your idea will give you negotiating power for the license. With your patent, you can demand for a higher royalty payment as you have brought down their upfront legal cost and minimised their risk. Your patent also gives them peace of mind that your idea or invention is completely original and that they will not have to enter into any legal battles with any person or business for patent infringement. In fact, most companies will only accept to hold a license for an idea or an invention that is patented.

Everybody would want to benefit from their invention fully and will also want to prevent others from using or selling their ideas without their full knowledge. You will not be able to achieve this if your product is not patented. In fact, without a patent, you are not really the owner of an invention or an idea. If another person steals your idea and patents it before you, it may be an exercise in futility to try to prove your ownership of the idea. So, when you patent an idea, you get an exclusive right over the product and will be able to stop others from using, selling and producing your idea/invention without your express permission. Patent rights also stop other people from copying or duplicating an invention as well as importing it unless the owner permits them.

A patent right is a veritable means through which you will be able to control the market. This is because when you have the patent, you are the sole determinant force in the market until your patent elapses.

Thus, you will be able to sell your product or invention at a price you want. In this way, you will be able to reap the fruit of your hard work.

If you own a patent over a product, you are at liberty to determine what becomes of the invention and how it should be utilised.

Your patent can be a good means of revenue. There are various ways through which you will be able to get money from a patent invention (idea). I have already talked about the first one. Here, a patent gives you the monopoly of the market as far as the item is concerned. You determine the price at which to sell. Besides, if you want to give yourself some rest and peace of mind that nobody will appropriate your idea, then you have to patent your product or idea. The implication is that you will be using, selling or producing your invention or idea alone until your patent period is over. You can also patent your idea and license it to another company or individual to sell, use or manufacture as the case may be. You will earn some money by collecting royalties accruing from the sales or use of your invention.

The Ugly Sides of Patenting an Idea

It is always said that what has an advantage also has a disadvantage. This applies to a patent. Patenting an idea comes with a number of disadvantages. Here are some of the disadvantages of obtaining patent rights.

First, patenting your idea or invention means revealing or disclosing the secret and details of your invention to the public, including your competitor. They can study your invention with the information you provide and then look for means of improving on it. Once, they come out with an improvement and patent it, you are likely going to lose business to your competitor as it is now better than yours.

It is also not easy to go to court with another person that violates your patent right. This is because the process and what are involved are time-consuming and expensive. The waiting time for the application to be processed can be very lengthy, especially if you apply for a utility patent. It is also an expensive process. Apart from the application fees, there are other expenses that you will incur such as the maintenance fee, the patent attorney fees, the cost for searching for existing patents and others. You will have to hire a very good and efficient lawyer to defend you in court against an infringer. This too is also an expensive project. You may not have enough money to pursue the case till the end.

A patent is territorial, meaning that its effects and advantages are limited to the jurisdiction where it is issued. Your invention can be abused and your right violated in other locations where the patent is not acknowledged. If you want to move and popularise your invention in other locations, it is recommended that you go the territory and seek for a new patent to enable you take full control of the market there.

Any person can utilise your invention or idea once your patent reaches its expiration date.

Patent, Trademarks, Copyrights and Servicemarks: What Are the Differences?

Inventors and owners of intellectual properties and other kinds of products are protected by the law against various kinds of theft, unlawful and unauthorised use of their works by other people. Some of these legal protections and rights are similar and can be confused with each other. But in reality, they are not the same. The ones that are most commonly acknowledged across the globe are trade, patent, copyright and servicemarks. In this subheading, I am going to examine these terms to show how they differ from each other.

Trademark and servicemark

The terms trademark and servicemark are almost the same and serve the same purpose. The major difference between the two is that while the former identifies the owner of a product and differentiates it from other similar products on the market, the latter identifies and differentiates an originator of a service from others. Sometimes, the term "trademark" can be used to mean trademark and servicemark as explained above. Typical examples of trademarks and servicemarks are logo and brand name. Examples of businesses that make use of trademarks are electronic and mobile device business. But such business as insurance, transportation and food service industries use servicemark because these are services and not products. However, it is possible for a business to have both a trademark and servicemark. For example, a restaurant offers food services. But they also sell food as their products. They need trademark to sell their products and servicemarks to offer their services.

Trademark/servicemark does not have any expiration period. It lasts forever because it is the usage that bestows the right on the owner. As far as you are using the trademark, it will not expire. In a similar manner, there is no expiration to the registration of a trademark insofar as you keep to the terms such as paying fees at regular intervals and filing specific documents. Each country has its unique trademark/servicemark, laws even though the principles are similar.

A patent I have explained above gives an exclusive right to an inventor to use, import and sell their invention which may be a product, process, ideas, structural mechanism, appearance, asexually produced plants, and others. The right is given to encourage inventiveness and creativity and also to ensure that the inventor gets full benefit of their invention at least within a specified period of time. Unlike trademark/servicemark, this right does not last forever. It is given for a limited period after which other people can use, sell or produce the invention.

Copyright is another type of right given to intellectual property owners. This type of right is given to the author of original works such as musical, artistic, dramatic and literary works such as novels, poetry, architecture, computer software, songs and movies. Like a patent and unlike trademark/servicemark, the right is not an everlasting right. But its duration is more complex than that of a patent as a number of factors are taken into consideration in order to determine it. This explains why all literary works do not have the same duration. Its practice also differs from country to country. For example, in the US, the copyright protection for a work of an individual will continue throughout the life of the person and ends at 70 years after his or her demise. But that of an anonymous publication will last for 95 years starting from the publication date or 120 years from the date it was created depending on which one is shorter.

The table below will make the difference between these terms much easier to understand.

Points of differences	Copyright	Patents	Trademark/Servicemark
What the right secures	Copyright protects original works of authorship like photographs, paintings, recordings, pictures, motors, songs, articles, books of different kinds, sculptures and other literary and artworks	Patent right secures inventions including structural and mechanical functionality, processes, machines, composition of matters, designs, asexually produced plants, manufactures and others.	Protects logos, symbols, designs, words, phrases and the likes which stands for and marks the source of the goods out from other party.
Requirements to be protected	Copyright can only protect original and creative work which has to be created on a material item or something that can be touched or felt.	It only secures usable, novel and nonobvious inventions.	For a mark to be protected by trademark/service mark, it has to be unique implying that it should separate the source of a product/service from others.

Points of differences	Copyright	Patents	Trademark/Servicemark
Protection's terms	Depends on jurisdiction that grants it	Depends on a jurisdiction issuing it	It normally lasts as long as it is being used.
Rights Granted	Right to take charge of the production, reproduction, selling/ distribution, display and public performance of copyrighted works as well as derivative works.	Right to exclude others from selling, importing, making or using patented ideas or inventions.	Right to utilise the symbol/mark and stop others from making use of such marks in such a manner that will result in confusion about the goods'/services' origin.

Chapter Two: The Legal Implication of A Patent

Patent rights are given to encourage innovation, creativity and inventiveness. It is a kind of inducement or reward to people who are able to invent useful novel and nonobvious things, processes, designs, plants and, chemical and material compositions and others. However, enforcing this right to the full and in all circumstances is likely to turn against the ultimate objective of the patent system, which is to improve public welfare. In order to protect the interest of inventors and ensure that the ultimate goal of the system is still met, virtually all jurisdictions across the globe put some limitations on the enforcement of the patent law. Thus, there may be certain limitations and certain exceptions to this exclusive right in each country. If you are applying for a patent in a country, it is therefore pertinent that you find out what the exceptions and limitations are.

Each country is unique in this regard and as such, it may be difficult to discuss patent limitation and exception of all countries separately. However, there are aspects of these limitations that are almost general for all countries. I will take a look at these general aspects as explained by SCP.

Private and/or non-commercial use: Most jurisdictions across the globe do not forbid their citizens from making use of patented inventions in private and for non-commercial purpose. In my thinking, this exemption makes sense, as it is the only means through which other creative minds will be able to improve on the inventions of others. If the patent exclusive rights forbid personal and non-commercial use of patented works, there is no way other creative minds will be able to study an existing invention in order to improve on that. Besides, if private use of patented work is not allowed by patent laws, it means that inventors will use their works by themselves, which gives them no benefit.

Experimental Use and/or Scientific Research: Patent exclusive rights do not forbid scientists and researchers from studying or carrying out research on patented work. As I mentioned above, allowing this limitation is a way of encouraging inventiveness, research and creativity. In fact, most inventions would not have been made if patent exclusive rights prevent people from carrying out research or studying patented inventions. Many inventions are made in the course of study of another invention.

Exhaustion of patent rights: The exclusive rights granted in a patent is not everlasting. It has a validity period which is twenty years in the US and UK (for the UK, it has to be renewed every 5 years for 20 years). Once the right expires, other producers or individuals can begin to produce, sell or import the product. This does not deny the inventor the right to benefit from their invention. This is because the patent right owner is expected to have utilised their exclusive right very well and make a lot of money. This is why a patent validity period for most countries is very large or up to 20 years.

Extemporaneous preparation of medicines: Patented work can be used to prepare medicine insofar as there is no prior plan to use the invention for such a purpose.

Acts for getting regulatory approval: Many jurisdictions include clauses in their patent laws that give relevant regulatory bodies and agencies the right to give permission or approve the use of patented works. But such use is normally controlled. There are a number of reasons why a firm, an individual or business establishments may be allowed by a relevant governmental body and agencies to use a patented work. It can be for research or study purpose. It could be for the interest of the public. However, there are always requirements to satisfy before such an approval is granted.

Compulsory licensing and/or government use: The patent laws of a lot of countries allow their government or agencies the full right of usage over patented work insofar as such usage will benefits the public.

Certain use of patented works by breeders and farmers: Farmers and breeders for the interest of the entire society may be allowed to utilised certain aspects of patented invention for a particular purpose.

Prior use: The patent law in many countries does not prevent people from using unpatented works or forbid the use of any work before it is patented.

Use of articles on foreign vessels, land vehicles and aircrafts: Patent limitation and exceptions also include the use of articles on foreign vessels, aircrafts and land vehicles.

As I mentioned above, there are no universally accepted patent laws. Each country has her own patent regulations. The same thing applies to the limitation and exception to the exclusive rights granted in patent. What are given above are certain aspects that are common in most patent laws. So, you need to find out what is obtainable in your location in this regard.

Patent Validity

Patent rights, when granted, are not dogmas that cannot be challenged or that you cannot file a protest against. In other words, the validity of any patent can be challenged. There are two issues concerning patent validity. First, a person can initiate a legal procedure for the annulment of your validly granted patents rights. Secondly, you can also challenge the validity of patent rights or ask a court to annul it. In any of the above cases, the court considers several factors in order to determine the validity of a patent.

It is not an easy process to invalidate a patent. The appellant is required to prove beyond reasonable doubt that the patent right should not have been granted in the first instance due to the failure of the patent owner to meet the statutory requirements for the granting of patents. For example, the validity of a patent can be challenged on the ground that it is nonobvious (in the US) or does not involve an inventive step, as it is the case in Europe. The problem is establishing and proving your case.

For any evidence to stand in a patent validity case, it should have occurred before the patent application is made. You don't provide proof or facts that occurred after the patent application is launched. In this case, your statement lacks strength, as it is not supported with prior art.

Prior art in this regard means any material disclosed to the public before the patent application or any relevant date of a patent. So, before you apply for patent rights, it is recommendable that you carry out a prior art search to find out if any publication has been made on the same invention prior to the filing of your application. For the publication to serve as a prior art, it has to be the same or contain all aspects of your claimed inventions indicating that your invention is no longer a novel invention. Therefore, your patent is not right.

In many countries like in Europe, the date considered as the relevant date is the date the patent application is made. However, in the US, the relevant date is the date of invention. So, when you are performing a patent validity search, you should also consider the relevant date as it will be your guide and canon to determine whether your patent is valid or not or whether another person's patent is valid or not.

If you discover during prior art search that there is a prior art or a publication has been made before the relevant date or before the date of invention depending on what is obtainable in your country, you have to do a comparison of the publication and your patent claims to determine their similarity and differences. It is of crucial importance that you examine each element contained in the independent claims separately. An independent claim refers to any claim that stands on itself without any reference or link to another claim. The next thing to do after examining all independent claims is to examine the dependent claims, which are the direct opposite of independent claims. If the prior art or publication contains all the independent claims, then you should not apply for any patent, as your invention is not new. However, if any of the independent elements is not contained in the publication, you can now apply for a patent for the one/those that are not mentioned in the prior art because it is or they are considered as novel and nonobvious.

Another important factor to take into consideration when challenging the validity of any patent is the time you are required to file a protest against a patent validity. It differs from country to country. For example, in Europe, to validly initiate a court case for the invalidation of any patent right, the protest must be lodged within nine months from the date the patent is granted. If the patent law of your country requires you to file for the invalidation of a patent within a specified period of time, you should ensure that you lodge your application during the timeframe allowed by the law otherwise your application can be knocked out by the court as lacking merit.

Patent Infringement

The term patent infringement refers to the violation of the patent rights of another person. It comes into play when a person or an entity uses, imports, produces or sells an idea or invention protected by a patent. People can easily infringe on other people's patent right, either intentionally or not. Such an infringement is legally frowned at and can result in a huge penalty or fine if the patent owner seeks for redress in court. However, it is easy to catch an infringer but not very easy to prove such a case in court. Here, I am going to tell you what to do when your patent right is violated. Before going into that, let us first examine the various kinds of patent infringement.

Types of patent infringement

A patent can be infringed on in four different ways. Below are four different kinds of patent infringement that you should know or look out for if you have a patented invention.

Direct infringement: This means exactly what it sounds like. In this type of patent infringement, the infringer uses, manufactures and imports patented items/inventions/ideas without any authorisation from the patent owner. The violation may be out of ignorance or wilfully.

Indirect infringement: In this type of patent infringement, the infringer is not involved in a direct sell, use or manufacture of a patent item or invention but helps another person to use, sell, or make patented work. A person can also be guilty of this type of infringement by encouraging or inducing another person to violate another person's patent right.

Contributory Infringement: This type of infringement occurs when a person provides a patented work to another person, (a direct infringer) knowing fully well that it is a patented item. This type of infringement is a form of indirect infringement also.

Literal Infringement: The patent claims describe or define an invention. If another person comes up with an invention that corresponds with or that is exactly what the patent claims define, the person is guilty of literal infringement.

Note that in some jurisdictions, there may be more kinds of patent infringement. It is the scope of the patent law of a country that will determine what is regarded as patented infringement. For example, the United States of America's patent laws give room for non-literal patent infringement. In other words, an invention may violate a patented invention even though it does not have a literal correspondence with the patent claims of another invention. Let's take a brief look at the patent infringement laws of various countries.

Patent Infringement Legislations of Different Countries

Canadian patent infringement

The patent legislation in Canada is enshrined in the Canadian Patent Act. The s.42 stipulates the rights of the patent holder by excluding others from using, making, selling, or constructing a patented invention. The Canadian Patent Act favours the patent holder in a number of ways. First, it does not oblige them to provide any prior art as the basis for the validity of a patent. You cannot invalidate a patent in Canada because of the absence of a prior art. A patent infringement case is normally handled by a judge rather than by a jury, as it is the case in the US. It is less time consuming and more cost effective to pursue a patent violation case in Canada than in the US because the country has a more streamlined discovery process. There is also an implied undertaking rule governing its discovery process and this does not allow the utilisation of information obtained or revealed during the discovery for any other reasons except for the purposes of court case for which is revealed. The complainant has the right to decide whether to demand for compensation for damages suffered or to claim an accounting of profits. In Canadian patent infringement cases, punitive damages are hardly awarded while treble damages are unknown in the Canadian courts.

Australia

Australian patent infringement law forbids both direct and indirect violation of the patentee's right by the unauthorised use, make, sell or construction of their invention. The term exploit used by the law to refer to the unauthorised use of the patentee's work can mean a lot of things. It can be used to mean the selling, hiring, making, importation of a patented item or even the disposal or damaging of a patented product without the patentee's authorisation. The importation or use of patented product without the authorisation of a patent holder is also against the law. The law also forbids the of use of patented process or methods. You can initiate a legal process against any person that violates any of these Australian patent laws.

Europe

The European Patent Office is the institution that gives inventors the exclusive patent rights. However, patent infringement issues are handled by each country or member-state. There is no unified patent court that centrally enforces patent infringement. But in the recent time, some member countries have agreed to establish a unified patent court to handle patent violation issues. This court is yet to start functioning.

United Kingdom

Section 60 of the UK Patent Act 1977 as amended defines what constitutes patent infringement in the country. The section forbids production, disposition of and importation of a patented product or invention. Patent infringement in the UK also includes providing or offering to provide patented product or invention to any person that is not authorised to use it. UK patent law also punishes any person that disposes or offers to dispose of a patent invention or product. I shall discuss the UK patent laws in detail later in this book.

The United States of America

In the United States of America, there is both direct and indirect patent infringement. A person violates a patent directly by using, selling, producing, importing or offering to sell a patented invention, product or its equivalent. On the other hand, a person can indirectly violate a patentee right by causing, influencing or inciting others to directly commit patent infringement.

In the US, patentees may not be allowed to file any patent infringement case unless a patent is issued. However, as I shall show in the relevant section below, under 35 U.S.C. paragraph 154, a patent applicant can be issued with pre-grant protection against certain forms of infringement that will occur before a full patent right is granted to him. A person with the pre-grant protection can file for patent infringement and be awarded with considerable amount of royalty as compensation for some types of infringing activities. To get the compensation, the plaintiff has to prove that infringement was committed after the patent application has been published. The patent claims should also be same in substance with the claims in the published application. The applicant also has to prove that the infringer was aware of the published patent application.

Protecting Oneself or Business Against Patent Infringement

Sometimes, some businesses and individuals don't violate patent rights intentionally. But in the face of the law, there is no distinction between inadvertent and intentional violation of a patent right. Once you violate another person's right, you can be sued and if found guilty, you will be slammed with the required penalty. To be on the safer side, it is advisable that you protect yourself or business against patent infringement. Getting patent infringement insurance is a veritable means of achieving this.

Patent infringement insurance provides coverage to an inventor or a third party against unintentional violation of another person's patent right. If an inventor who may be a business or an individual obtains patent infringement insurance, the insurance company will take care of any legal fees incurred when the inventor sues an infringer for the violation of their patent rights. But if a third party who is covered by patent infringement insurance is issued by an inventor for the violation of their patent rights, the insurance company will take care of the legal cost for the case.

It is very expensive to pursue a patent infringement case. Depending on the type of business and type of infringement involved, it can run into millions of dollars or pounds. Given this, the premium charged by the patent insurers are normally very high and the total cost of such insurance is also very high that many people do not consider it to be worth doing.

What to do when your patent rights are infringed

If you own a validly granted patent and you think that another person has infringed on your right, you can proceed to the court for your right to be enforced and probably to seek for compensation for the violation of your right. However, as I mentioned above, it is not an easy legal process to prove patent infringement. The process involves a number of things, which definitely requires you to hire a lawyer proficient in handling patent rights. Here are things to do in order to prove that your patent has been infringed on or to deny any accusation of patent infringement.

Validity Search

The first thing to do when you discover that your patent right has been infringed on or violated is to do a patent validity search, which is almost the same as prior art search. The major difference between them is the intention for which they are carried out. Prior art search aims at discovering if there is any publication or invention before the relevant date. But patent validity search, which is also called invalidity search, is carried out in order to protect one patent validity and proves another invalid. In other words, in patent validity search, you are looking for prior art that will support the nullification of another rival patent. You may need an expert to help you in this regard. Once you are able to find a prior art for the cancellation of the targeted patent, you can move on to another stage in the enforcement of your patent right, which is claims chart mapping.

The benefits of patent validity search

Performing a patent validity search will give you a number of benefits. First, it is a veritable means of enhancing your business to a considerable extent. If you are accused of patent infringement, a validity search is the only way to show that there is a prior art before the relevant date of the patent you are accused of violating. On the other hand, you can also use it to prove that your patent rights have been violated by another person. Your ability to perfectly prove an allegation of patent infringement to be false or to show that another infringes your patent rights is a plus to your business or yourself as it solidifies your intellectual property portfolio and increases its value. This statement is correct whether you plan on selling, using or licensing your intellectual property.

When you have a solid intellectual property, you can establish a strong reputation on it. You will not fall into the snare of your rivals and NPE. If you are their target, they will end up wasting their resources and time, as they will not get you. Definitely, your competitors will know that you have a strong intellectual property and patent portfolio, the number of them that will be on the lookout for infringement on your own side will reduce and this will give you a peace of mind that you are an object of nobody's target. It is a deterrent to NPEs as they will not find anything that will warrant sending you a demand letter.

Claim chart mapping

Claim chart mapping involves the analysis of the infringement during which the claims in a patent are evaluated. Claim chart mapping differs from invention description, as it is possible for it to be modified during the application process. This is because most claimants enlarge the level of their coverage and include more than what they are granted. They will gradually modify their claims when they are told that they are requesting for more than what can be granted legally to them.

It is of crucial importance to properly and thoroughly examine the claims. This will help you to understand and to figure out where your prior art will be relevant. This is important whether you think your patent right has been infringed on by another person or whether you want to show that you didn't violate any person's patent rights.

Demand letter

The next thing to do is to write down your legal claims and request for compensation in a letter known as a demand letter. You can issue a demand letter to an infringer, which could be a company, a non-practicing entity (NPE) or an individual. Similarly, any person including a company and an individual can also issue a demand letter to you. NPE do not make anything or render any service. However, they acquire intellectual property rights like patents and make money from them by utilising them as a basis for initiating a court case.

Violating the patent right of a NPE is not a good case at all. This is because they will always want to enforce their rights to its fullest because they are interested in the gain they will make from it. They will want all negotiations to be as they want it. So, the best thing to do is to avoid them by all means or avoid doing anything that will make them go after you. This entails that you have a solid intellectual property package, which will require an excellent claims chart mapping process.

Patent Enforcement

Patent right infringement can be taken to court for redress and adequate compensation. It is important for you to know that patent grantors are not their enforcers. It is the court that enforces a patent right. So, if your patent right is violated and you want to enforce it, you take the infringer to court. This is a standard practice for the majority of the countries across the globe, even the process of initiating a litigation against an infringer may be different. Here are the steps to follow when filing a patent for patent enforcement.

- Getting a good lawyer

Patent infringement cases are difficult cases and require reliable and strong legal representatives. It is not a type of case that will be handled by any lawyer. Sometimes, people lose their cases and even incur more expenses because they don't have a strong and experienced legal team. To avoid spoiling your case, it will be wise that you hire a law firm that specialises in handling International Property infringement cases. In patent infringement, it should be the first thing to do. This is because you will be working in collaboration with your lawyer in every other step mentioned below to ensure that you are properly guided.

- Carrying out a pre-suit investigation

Before you initiate any legal procedure against an infringer, it is recommended that you carry out a pre-suit investigation and make all necessary investigations to find out how strong your case will be against an infringer or the possibility of you winning the legal battle with an infringer. The defendant will put up a strong defence against the complainant in the court. So, as a plaintiff, you should be able to prove your case before a jury or judge, depending on what is obtainable in your area. It is possible to have a strong case against an infringer but lose it due to lack of evidence as a result of insufficient pre-suit investigation.

The process of pre-suit investigation is part of what I have discussed above in patent validity. In your pre-suit investigation, you have to do the following things and ensure that they are properly done.

Draft your infringement claim charts. This means juxtaposing each claim against each item, method/process or device that you suspect violates your patents.

- Take a second and hard look at the prior art search

Consider the possibility of the accused filing an inter partes review or re-examination of the patent of the company and how successful it is likely going to be.

It is also of crucial importance that you review the business activities of the accused infringer. Here, you have to determine not only the sales but also the potential damages.

You should also take time to have a discussion with the patented product's inventor as well as other chief witness. This will enable you to ascertain its features, possibility of success, weakness and strengths.

Pre-suit investigation is a veritable means through which a company will acquire additional information and details about an allegation of patent infringement before approaching the court. Armed with these details, the legal representative of your company will prepare very well to overcome the defence team of the defendant. This is also the stage to gather and keep all necessary documents and evidence secure before the matter goes to the court for determination. If you go through this stage painstakingly, the discovery process will be much easier and smoother. You will also be in a better position to determine whether or not you will be successful.

- A cease-and-desist letter may quell the fire

If your company does not have enough money or is not financially strong to pursue a patent infringement litigation, it will be in your interest to write a cease-and-desist letter to the infringer informing them that they may be violating your patent rights. This approach is a veritable means of initiating friendly negotiation and discussion between your company and the potential infringer. The resolution of the case between the patentee and the would-be patent infringer will ensure that no court case is initiated. On the other hand, the potential infringer may also decide to approach the court to declare that the patent is not valid meaning that it does not violate any person's patent right. In this situation, you will become the defendant rather than the plaintiff. Given this, if your company is not ready to engage any business in any patent related litigation, the person should send the cease-and-desist letter. You can only send this letter if you are ready and willing to engage a potential infringer in a legal battle.

Based on this, some people do not consider sending a cease-and-desist letter a good idea. They discourage this because they believe that if an infringer goes to court to file for a declaratory judgment, they will gain certain tactical advantage, as you will be on the defensive side. However, no matter how plausible their argument may be, a cease-and-desist letter still remains a peaceful and more cost effective means of settling a patent infringement case out of court. You may not even spend a dime depending on whether your cease-and-desist letter is written by a lawyer or yourself.

- Set up a plan for the lawsuit

After doing the second step mentioned above and the infringer refuses to settle amicably with you or prefers a litigation, you have no other option than to welcome the challenge. However, before engaging in a legal battle, it is of crucial importance that you set up a strong plan for the lawsuit. There are a number of factors that you should take into consideration while preparing your litigation plan. Here are some of the things to consider when planning for the litigation.

- Make a budget for the lawsuit

It is good that you make a budget for the patent infringement court case. As I have mentioned above, it is an expensive exercise. It is not something that you should embark on without having sufficient funds for it. So, having a budget will help you to determine whether you are financially capable of the battle. When making your budget, ensure that you cover the cost for the filing of the case as well as the legal cost for the trial process and other miscellaneous and other logistics. You should also consider lawyer's fees if you are not using your company's lawyers.

A profound understanding of possible proofs that may be countered by your legal teams and the infringer's legal representative is essential. You should also consider additional evidence that may be required to back up your claims. It is also important that you try to figure out the possible evidence the infringer will provide as a support for his case.

Your plan should also include a strategy to use in pursuing the case. This strategy should take into consideration a discovery plan and possible motions your legal teams and the defence group will bring up.

Note that enforcing your patent right can be very expensive but it gives some advantages, especially if the case eventually turns to your favour. For example, it is a veritable means of resolving the issue permanently. Once the court gives a verdict to your favour, the case is over and your company's interest in the market will be protected. However, the reverse can also be the case when the case favours the accused infringer.

Patent Enforcement Dos and Don'ts

Patent enforcement cases are quite different from other kinds of litigations. What applies to other kinds of court cases may not apply in patent infringement cases. Consequently, when you are planning and strategizing on how to file a lawsuit against an infringer, there are some dos and don'ts to take into consideration. Here are some of them.

- Don't think you need to implement your patent to be able to enforce it

If your invention is patented but you're yet to turn it into a product/service, you will still be able to sue any infringer. Non-implementation of a patented idea does not nullify the exclusive right granted to the inventor. Such an inventor is seen as a non-practicing entity. Unless your patent duration has expired, you have the right to enforce it whether you have implemented your invention or not.

- Don't be afraid to enforce your patent

Some people are afraid to enforce their patent because they were told that patent enforcement cases are expensive. There are also another group of people that will fold their hands and watch others use their patents because they don't want to send them a cease-and-desist letter to avoid any possible declaratory judgment by the suspected infringer. If you don't enforce your patent, you will not gain anything from it as other people will definitely usurp your patent and rip you of the benefits you are supposed to gain from it. Once you notice that somebody is violating your patent right, you need to act quick. Don't delay action because of lack of money or any other reason. Strike a deal with a patent enforcement company to manage and fund the lawsuit for you. At the end of the process, you will give them their own share of what comes out of the entire deal.

- Don't fail to patent your invention as soon as they are made

If you make any invention, go through the steps mentioned above on patent validity to ensure that no other person has invented such a thing. Once you are sure that the invention has not been registered, you should immediately patent your invention. Any delay here can be dangerous. This is because there is the possibility for a competitor to make the same invention or even copy yours and patent it before you. Once it is patented, the credit will go to them. You are no longer the owner of the patent. Even if you don't want to practice or implement your patent, you can license it to another company and get paid in the form of royalty.

- Don't draft your patent claims by yourself

Many inventors create problems for themselves by drafting their own patent or trying to prosecute it by themselves. This is not a good idea even if you are talented, you need to hire a professional service to handle that for you. This is because patent claims are legal documents which exclude others from selling, importing or making your inventions. You need to capture all aspects and features of your inventions in your patent otherwise you will make them unenforceable. It is not enough to have patent. To make your patent stronger, you should have well-crafted patent claims. In summary, if your patent claims are not properly constructed, your rights will also suffer.

Similarly, it is a bad idea to represent one's self in court for cases of patent infringement. Patent infringement cases are complicated in almost all countries across the globe. It is also expensive. Given its complex nature, it is a bad idea to handle it by yourself, or to use an attorney that does not specialise in IP litigations. So, don't handle it by yourself even if you are a lawyer unless you are experienced in such a case.

- Indicate your patent number(s) on your products

If you have already turned your patented invention into a product or a service, ensure that your patent number is clearly written on your service or product. This is a veritable means of informing the public that your product/service is patented and nobody should infringe on that. It serves the same purpose as a cease-and-desist letter but it does not have the same consequences with it. With it, you will avoid the possibility of an infringer filing for a declaratory judgement. It is a constructive way of warning an infringer. Ensure that your patent numbers appear on the user-manual or any other paperwork that accompanies your product and also on your product.

- Remove the patent number from your products and user-manual at the expiration of your patent

Once the validity period of your patent elapses, it is necessary that you remove the number from all your products and any other paperwork that accompanies it which contains the patent number. In some jurisdictions, inventors that don't remove their patent numbers from their products/services can be sued by individuals on behalf of the government. So, to avoid facing such a lawsuit, you should abide by this instruction.

- Apply for your patent right on time

Once you have an invention, apply for its patent right. Don't delay, as it can be dangerous. Bear in mind that you are not the only person studying or researching. Another person may be researching on something that will lead into making a similar invention.

- See your patent as an asset

Patents are great assets and can give you lots of money if you gain the monopoly of the market. Even if you don't want to implement the patented invention, you can still make money from it by licensing it to another company or even selling it completely to another. This is why you should consider your patent as an asset.

This brings us to the end of this chapter and section. In the coming section, I will discuss patent rights as enshrined in the patent law of the United States of America.

Section Two: Patents in the United States of America

The United States of America has a unique patent law. If you want to seek for patent protection in the US, it is important that you abide by the patent requirements of the country as enshrined in the Patent Act (35 U.S. Code). This section is comprised of one chapter. It will take a look at some crucial aspects of the code so that you will have a good understanding of what the US patent law demands of you. In addition, the chapter provides some practical tips to help you apply for a patent and avoid unnecessary pitfall, errors and scams in the process of seeking for a patent.

Chapter Three: The Basics of US Patents

In this first chapter of this section, I am going to discuss the fundamentals of the US Patent Act. Note that what is discussed in this chapter is just the tip of the ice berg, because the US Patent Act is comprehensive and deals with a lot of issues concerning patents, which may be outside the scope of this book or too big for a book of this nature.

The United States Patent Office: Locations and Functions

If you are planning to patent your invention or idea in the US, you should know the office in charge of patents and their important contact details, as you will be contacting them often for one reason or the other. Here, I will tell you their contact details and other necessary information about the office and operations.

The first thing you should know is that a patent in the United States of America is issued by the United States Patent and Trademark Office which is commonly known by its acronym "USPTO." USPTO is under the U.S Department of Commerce. It has various wings through which it discharges its officially assigned duties. It is the responsibility of the agency to protect people's inventions by granting them the protection against unauthorised use of their inventions over a specified period of time. It is also their duty to register trademarks. Apart from registering trademarks and granting patents, this office also has other responsibilities, such as assisting and providing sound advice to the US government including the presidency, the Secretary of Commerce, various units of the Department of Commerce and other governmental agencies on issues relating to intellectual property both nationally and internationally. However, each of these functions of the agency are handled by a separate unit. In other words, each matter relating to IP is handled by a department of USPTO. Here, I am going to concentrate on the patent aspect of their function.

The USPTO receives and assesses applications from inventors seeking for patents to determine if they merit the exclusive rights. The office also grants patents to applicants that qualify for them. Apart from granting the patent, they also publish and circulate information relating to patents. It is also their duty to provide official records as well as copies of patents to the public when it is required. It falls within the scope of the function of the USPTO to document and maintain records of patents including foreign patents, and to keep records of assignment/transfer of patents. The search room utilised by the public to access issued patents and records is also managed and maintained by this agency of the US Department of Commerce. The USPTO issues the Manual of Patent Examining Procedure, which contains patent regulations and explains its requirements. The agency organises training sessions for the practitioners on the patent laws and requirements as contained in the book. The USPTO in discharging its functions helps the United States to preserve her technological dominance over other countries and this in turn helps her to remain on top of the competition in various aspects.

You can see from the above why you should know the office and what services they will offer you. But to avail yourself of the services of this office, you still need to know their contact details. Bear in mind that the patent department of the USPTO is not a one-office department. There are various units discharging different functions. For example, there are various technology centres (TCs) handling the assessment of applications for patents. When an application is refused, there is another unit of the USPTO where such refusal can be appealed against. Other functions discharged by different units include receiving and distributing mail, reviewing drawings, keeping records of assignment, handling sales of printed copies of patents, receiving new applications and many others. Majority of these units have their separate contact details. Here, I will not be providing the contact details of all the wings of the USPTO. Below are some of the important contacts you should know.

Website of the United States Patent Office: https://www.uspto.gov/.

Contact Centre for General Information

Toll-free: 800-786-9199

Local: 571-272-100

You can use the above number to obtain general information, make inquiries about addresses both mailing and Internet addresses, to get agency's accounts and to get other contact information of any unit of the agency or other support services. The number is available during the workday from 8:30am to 8:00p.m. But it is not available during federal holidays.

The Office of the Chief Communications

This is a very important office in the agency. It takes charge of all matters relating to internal and external communications and also manages the public affairs function of USPTO. You can reach the Chief Communications Officer through these contact details:

Local: 571-272-8400

Fax: 571-273-0340

Patents

The table below shows the contact number of certain offices of the USPTO that give useful information about various aspects of the patent process and other relevant patent help.

Office	Function	Contact number
Inventors Assistance Centre	Provides the public with patent information and services.	Toll-free: 800-786-9199 Local: 571-272-1000 TTY: 800-877-8339

Office	Function	Contact number
Application Assistance Unit	Assists inventors with patent applications and provides answers and solutions to their questions and concerns relating patent applications and pre-examination process.	Toll-free: 888-786-0101 Local: 571-272-4000 Email: HelpAAU@uspto.gov
Patent Cooperation Treaty (PCT) Helpdesk	It provides help and useful information on the process of patent cooperation treaty.	Local: 571-272-4300 available on weekdays from 8:30am to 5:00pm.
Patent Trial and Appeal Board	Handles appeals, against refusals of patent rights, unacceptable decision of the examiner, interferences and post-issuance challenges to patents.	Local: 571-272-9797 Fax: 571-273-0053
Patent Electronic Business Centre	Helps applicants to complete and submit their	Toll Free: 866-217-9197 Local: 571-272-4100

Office	Function	Contact number
	electronic patent application form, review their applications in Public and Private PAIR and other related support assistance.	Email: ebc@uspto.gov Available on weekdays from 6:00am to Midnight ET. Closed during Federal Holidays.

Mailing Addresses

Types of Matter	Mailing Address
Patent matters	Commissioner for Patents P.O. Box 1450 Alexandria, VA 22313-1450
Mail stop after final correspondence (mail to different mail stops should be mailed differently)	Mail Stop AF Commissioner for Patents P.O. Box 1450 Alexandria, VA 22313-1450
Mail Stop Assignment Recordation Services	Mail Stop Assignment Recordation Services Director of the U.S Patent and Trademark Office P.O. Box 1450 Alexandria, VA 22313-1450

The US Patent Laws

The United States of America is one of the countries across the globe with rich and well-developed patent laws. The patent laws of the country were not developed in a day or just one sitting of the Congress. The history of the US Patent Act dated back to more than three hundred years. Both the content of the law and its names have been modified and changed severally to meet the needs of the society at the time the modifications were made. The first documented patent law made in the US was enacted in 1790. Since then, it has been revised and managed by different agencies for a number of times. Given the age of the Patent Act of the US and the fact that it has been reviewed to meet the demand of the society, the US Patent Act is among the best as it captures virtually all aspects of the patent.

However, the foundation of the current patent laws of the US was laid in 1952 with the enactment of the Patent Act of 1952, which demands that an inventor must describe their invention and its infringement claims. The 1952 Patent Act also sets certain conditions that an invention must meet to be patentable. First, it has to be a novel/new invention. It also requires an invention to be useful and nonobvious (I have already explained the meaning of these terms in the preceding chapters, refer back to them in case you have forgotten) before it can be patented. The nonobvious requirement was added to ensure that individual inventors do not lay claims to or take advantage of the fundamental knowledge in a particular field.

No significant amendment was made to the US Patent Act since 1952 until 1999 and 2011 when the American Inventors Protection Act and Leahy-Smith America Invents Act were respectively enacted. The 1952 Patent Act was modified in each of these instances. However, the most significant among these major revisions was the 2011 America Invents Act. The debates that resulted in this significant 2011 review lasted for years. The focal point of the debate was whether patent rights should be granted to the person that first invents a product/process/method/design or to the person that first files for the patent right in the system. The arguments of the two sides were well examined with their pros and cons weighed thoroughly. After considering all the points, advantages and drawbacks of each side, the first-to-file system was adopted.

Before the adoption of the first-to-file, the 1952 Patent Act was based on the first-to-invent system. In other words, Leahy-Smith America Invents Act was mainly a switch from first-to-invent system to first-to-file. Other aspects of the 1952 Patent were largely retained by the AIA. The United States of America was among the last countries to accept the first-to-file patent system. But its application did not take effect until March 16, 2013.

Note that in the United States, only the Congress has the authority to make patent enactments. This power was bestowed on it by the Article 1, section 8 of the Constitution of the United States which states "Congress shall have power ... to promote the progress of science and useful arts, by securing limited times to authors and inventors the exclusive right to their respective writings and discoveries."

Important terms used in the Patent Act and their Meanings
The Patent Act of the US could be regarded as a legal document and thus some of the terms used there may mean something other than their conventional meanings. Thus, you need to give them the meaning attributed to them by the legislators. Below are a few of these terms, which will occur frequently in this book.
   ➢ Invention – It is used to mean invention or discovery.
   ➢ Process – The term process includes method, art and a new way of using an already known machine, process, material, composition of matter and manufacture.

➤ Patentee – Refers to the person to whom the patent rights was granted and also the successor of the person in the title to the patentee.

Types of Patent Allowed by the US Patent Law

In the US Patent law, the United States Patent and Trademark Office grants the patentee a property right to exclude other people from producing, utilising, selling, importing or offering for sale the patentee's invention(s). Normally, the patent term is a period of 20 years but under certain conditions, it can be extended or adjusted. Once the right is granted by the USPTO, it is the responsibility of the patentee to enforce their patent without any support from the grantor. In other words, the USPTO does not enforce patents. There are three types of patent rights granted under the United States of America Patent Act. I have explained each of them briefly above. This chapter is not intended to be a repeat of what has been said above but to take a more comprehensive look at them individually.

Utility Patents

Utility patent is also known as a patent of invention. It is the most common type of patent such that it has become synonymous with the term patent itself. Some people even use the terms patent and utility patent interchangeable. But the truth is that it is just a type of patent and does not define the US patent right in its entirety. This type of patent gives an exclusive right to any person that invents a new, useful and nonobvious machine, process, method, art, manufacture and new useful improvement on an existing invention. Any person that has an invention that does something useful is eligible to apply for this type of patent. Usefulness as defined by USPTO means anything that is capable of being used and that gives a recognisable benefit. Patent of Invention can be classified into three different types, namely, mechanical, chemical and electrical patents. Any invention belongs to any of these classifications. Pharmaceutical patents are a type of chemical patent.

What does the patent of invention protect?

Utility patent, or patent of invention, restrains other people from making, using, selling, importing or distributing a patented invention. However, you need to file and obtain the patent right to enjoy the protection. If you have an invention that qualifies for a patent, it is recommendable that you file for patent protection. As mentioned above, a patent right is given on the basis of first-to-file and not just first-to-invent.

How Long Does It Take to Get a Utility Patent?

When you file for a patent, the right is not granted immediately. This is because the patent application process goes through various stages. Besides, there are a number of factors that determine how long it takes for each of these stages to be accomplished. For a better understanding, I will give the time according to the various stages involved in the application process.

1. Patentability searching: This is the first stage of the application process. As I have explained above, before you lodge your application or before your application is processed by USPTO, a patentability search will be carried out to determine whether your invention is patentable or not. Through the search, it will be discovered if your invention meets the criteria for patents. This is the time to find out whether it is a novel, useful and nonobvious invention. Its validity is also determined here. Though USPTO performs the validity/patentable search internally, there are other private firms that offer the services to inventors planning to apply for a patent. It may take an office about 1 to 3 weeks to complete the patentability search. What determines how long it will take to complete the search are the volume of the search result and the amount of work the office has at the time you apply for the search.

2. Patent Application Drafting: Another important stage in the application process is the drafting of the application. As I have mentioned above, you have to describe your invention and your patent claims or its scope. This is work to be done by an expert or a legal firm that deals with patent rights and other intellectual property rights. Once you provide the firm with the required information about your invention, it may take about two weeks or a month for the application draft to be completed. It all depends on the proficiency of the person handling it, the complexity of the invention, the changes made after the drafting has started and the workload of the person preparing it. Once you have made the application draft, you can now file your application with USPTO, which is another process of its own.

3. Patent Application Filing: When you file your application, you will be given a "patent pending status." The time it will take for your application to be assessed and processed depend on the type of application you file. You can file for a provisional or non-provisional application. The provisional application takes a year longer to be processed than the non-provisional application. This is because a provisional application has to wait for a maximum of a year before it is changed into a non-provisional application. When it is changed to a non-provisional application, it has to undergo the same process of application that is made directly as non-provisional. It may take about 32 months or less than three years for USPTO to process a non-provisional application. Applications are assigned to various technical units and so the workload of the technical unit handling your application determines, to a certain extent, how long it will take for it to be processed. If waiting for up to three years is too much for you, the best option for you may be to prioritise the examination. But you should be able to meet the requirement before such service is given to you. The basic requirement is

the high fee required. Apart from the fee, it is only given to a limited number of applicants. If you apply for prioritised examination, your application will be processed within a period of one year.

Note that if you receive a patent pending status, you have not yet obtained the right. But nothing prevents you from making, selling, using and licensing your invention. The pending status is a warning sign to any person that may want to utilise your invention without your approval. Remember, the US patent law is carried out on the basis of first-to-apply.

The Duration of Patent of Invention

Patent of invention, when granted has a 20-year validity starting from the time the application was made. However, you need to be maintaining it during this periods by paying some fees. The maintenance fees are to be paid for the first time after 3.5 years from the time it is issued. Your second maintenance fees should be paid at 7.5 years from the issuance date and the third is paid at 11.5 years from the issue date. There is no surcharge during the six-month window period following each of the due dates, that is six months before the due date of the payment of the maintenance fee. When making the payment for the maintenance, you need to include your patent name and application number. Note that your patent will expire prematurely if you fail to pay your maintenance fees six months after the maintenance period expires. If you are paying during the grace period, you have to pay some surcharge as well. Bear in mind that the USPTO will not send you any notification email or mail for the payment of the maintenance fee. But you may be reminded to make your payment during the grace period. Your patent expires after the expiration of the grace period.

Design Patent

Design patent right is meant to secure the appearance or visual ornamental qualities of an item. According to USPTO, a design patent application's subject matter may relate to the article's form, configuration, to the surface ornamentation applied to an article or to the combination of the surface ornamentation and configuration due to the fact that a design inheres on an article of manufacture and cannot exist in isolation from it or cannot be separated from it. The structural or utilitarian features are not covered by a design patent. As mentioned above, a design patent granted by the USPTO protects only the appearance. For a design patent to be accepted, the design has to be an original, new and ornamental design.

A design patent may form the entire item or just part of it or one that is applied to the article. For this type of patent to be granted, its drawing must show how it is applied to the article. The drawing should also show the article in broken lines as it is without the design. Basically, there are two kinds of design patent applications.
You may file for a single claim design patent. However, a separate application should be lodged for independent and distinct design patent claims. They should not be included in a single patent claim. Independent designs are designs applied on different articles that have no relationship or any semblance. A typical example of such articles that have no apparent relationship are a car and a necklace. You must file separate applications for each of them. Designs of different forms and looks apply on different but related items that are considered to be distinct designs. Examples are two cars with a different look as a result of different surface ornamentation. However, USPTO may allow a single application for articles with little configuration differences or for modified forms, or

embodiments of a single design concept. Read more about this kind of design patent application from the Patent Act 37.

There is the tendency for some people to confuse a design patent with a utility patent. They are not the same because they do not protect the same thing. As stipulated in the US Patent Act, an inventor can apply for both utility and design patent as two of them protect two different things. While utility patents protect the operational mechanism and usage of an article, the design patent is meant to protect its ornamental appearance. However, the difference between these two patents is very subtle because it is not easy to separate the design of an article from its function and usage. They both determine each other.

Applying for a design patent

To apply for a design patent, there are some charges that you will be required to pay. The charges include the filing fee, search fee and examination. The amount to be paid depends on the status of the application. A non-profit organisation, a small business and an independent inventor or any applicant regarded as a small entity are charged only 50% of the actually amount bigger entities pay. The fees are specified on the Patent Search Fees section of the website of USPTO. The basic filing fee for a design patent is $200 (£143.16) but small entities are charged $100 (£71.58). It is further reduced to $50 (£35.79) for a micro entity. The USPTO design search fee is $160 (£114.53) but small entities and micro entities are respectively charged $80.00 (£57.26) and $40.00 (£42.95). Besides these, there are other fees that you are required to pay. Visit https://www.uspto.gov/learning-and-resources/fees-and-payment/uspto-fee-schedule to know other charges and the amount you are required to pay. However, bear in mind that most legal firms charge extra money or have their unique prices, if you hire them to help you with the application process. But even if you are going to use the services of a professional, it is recommended that you know the actual price charged by USPTO. This will help you to know when you are being overcharged by a legal firm.

For a design patent application to be granted, there are certain requirements the design is required to satisfy. The first thing you should bear in mind is that a design patent is only granted for an article to the extent that the functional features are dominated by the ornamental features. Secondly, such a design must be repeatable. Methods (including the methods of applying a design) are not protected by a design patent. They come under patent of invention. Just like the utility patent, a design patent must be original and should also meet ornamental standards. The design should be nonobvious when assessed from the point of view of ornamental features. A design patent has to also satisfy the criterion of novelty in the sense that prior art should not contain any identical designs. In addition, ornamental features that cannot be seen when an article is being used cannot be protected by a design patent. The subject of any design patent application is required to result from artistic conception and aesthetic skill. In other words, it will be difficult for you to acquire a patent for items that have no aesthetic appeal. A typical example of such an item is a rivet machine.

The term of a design patent starts counting from the time it is granted, which is unlike the term of patent of invention, which starts from the time the application for it is filed. In all, it normally expires after a period of 14 years.

As mentioned above, it is possible for you to obtain both design and utility patent rights for one invention. However, if you apply for utility and design patent rights, each of them will be examined differently and each is expected to satisfy all the stipulated requirements before they are granted. None are granted on the merit of the other. Also bear in mind, there are rules guiding against this type of coverage in order to avoid the issuance of two patents for one invention.

It may also be possible for you to secure copyright protections for a design regarded as a work of art. This depends on the extent the subject of a design patent is regarded as a work of art. Again, if the design inheres in a tangible item, it can also be granted a trademark right, especially if the physical article serves as a trademark.

As it is the case with other kinds of patent, the design patent provides the inventor an exclusive right to sell, use and make use of an article that has the same look or appearance with the patented design. In other words, the design patent forbids other people from applying a patented design to a product that looks like the product on which the patented design inheres such that an ordinary observer may confuse the infringing product with the patented product. The US Supreme Court established the standard for the ordinary observer in 1872 when it decided on a case that involved an ornamental design for silverware handles. The term "an ordinary observer" is used to refer to a retail consumer of the product in question and not an expert.

Bear in mind that the infringing product and the patented product are not juxtaposed in order to determined their difference and similarities. The test is more of a practical one with a hypothetical ordinary observer who goes out to purchase a patented design that he/she is fully aware of, but mistakes the infringing product with the original because it has the same appearance with the original. The ordinary consumer should also have made the purchase with full concentration. Another important aspect of the test to determine when a patented design is violated is that the two articles are to be compared as they will appear in their normal usage, which may not be the same as they appear when they are packaged and put in a carton.

To determine a design patent infringement, one must show that the various features of the patented design that are not contained in the prior art and also show that one or two of these features are applied on the infringing product. Failure to show this means that no infringement occurs. Another test will be carried out if any of the features is appropriated by the infringing product. In the second test, the uniqueness and similarities of the two articles will be examined to the extent they look alike and whether any existing similarity is strong to make an ordinary observer unable to differentiate them. If the similarity cannot deceive an ordinary consumer, then there is no infringement.

If you are applying for a design patent, you should ensure that your application has the following elements:

1. It must have an introductory part, which should contain the applicant's name and the title of the design. You must also briefly describe the nature of the product and the use you intend to put the article on which the design inheres on.
2. The application data sheet does not contain a cross-reference to the related applications.
3. A statement regarding research or development with federal sponsorship.
4. The applicant must describe the figures of the drawing in their application.
5. The application should describe the features of the design.
6. The claim is an important aspect of the application.
7. The applicant should support their application with the required drawings and photographs.
8. The application should also have the executed oath or declaration.

An application may be refused if any of these elements are missing. So, to ensure that you file a complete application or one that contains all the required elements, you should consider hiring an expert or a legal firm that specialises in handling issues relating to intellectual properties such as patents. Even though this will cost you some money, it will serve your interest.

Plant Patent

The United States Patent and Trademark Office grants protection to plant breeders who have reproduced distinct and new types of plants through an asexual means of production. The plants that exist naturally in an uncultivated state or plants propagated via tubers are excluded from plant patents. The term asexual reproduction refers to reproduction of plants without using fertilised seeds to ensure that the newly reproduced plant has the same genetic constitution with the parent plant. There are different means through which a plant can be asexually reproduced. Such means include rooting, layering, division, runners, apomictic seeds, corms, slips, rhizomes, bulbs, grafting and budding, tissue culture and nucellar embryos.

There are certain specific requirements which a plant must meet before it can be patented. For an invention to be protected by a plant patent, its subject matter must be a plant developed or discovered by a plant breeder and which can be propagated by asexual reproduction as proof of its stability. The inventor, whose name appears on the application, should actually be the person that developed, discovered, isolated or identified and reproduced it asexually. Plants excluded by the statues are not patentable. Any plant that has been made available to the public, patented before, or that has been put on sale or been in public use is also not patentable. The law also does not grant a patent to any plant described in a US patent or published patent application (there are exceptions to this rule). Additionally, a plant patent is granted to only inventors or discoverers of plants that are different from other known plants or plants that are related in characteristics to other plants. Differences resulting from the fertility level of the soil, environmental and growing conditions are not considered. The invention should also be nonobvious to a person with no skill in the art from the time of the filing of the patent claim. Apart from these specific requirements contained in Section 161 of

Title 35 United States Code, for an application for plant patent to be successful, it has to satisfy all general requirements for patentability. If you are not sure about anything regarding the patentability of your plant, you should seek the services of a professional.

Before you apply for a plant patent, you will be required to first carry out the asexual reproduction earlier before the filing of the application so that there will be enough time for USPTO to assess the clones, or propagules, of the claimed plant in order to determine its stability. This will give the evaluator the assurance that the reproduced plant has the same distinguishing qualities with the original plant.

Applying for a Plant Patent

If you are planning to apply for a plant patent, it is necessary that you visit the website of USPTO. You will find detailed information about the various fees such as filing, search and examination fees for plant patents. The code that deals with plant patents is 35 U.S.C 161. Visit it at http://www.uspto.gov/web/offices/ac/qs/ope/fees.htm to read more about these regulations.

The USPTO also permits inventors seeking for plant patents to hire a registered patent attorney or agent to help them with their application. Assignees seeking for this type of patent are required by law to use the services of a patent practitioner. The USPTO does not render any help when it comes to choosing an attorney or any agent. However, the agency requires all applicants using an agent or an attorney to hire one registered with them. You will find a list of registered attorneys and agents in the USPTO's online directory. Visit https://oedci.uspto.gov/OEDCI/practitionerRoster.jsp to view the list.

The application requirements and process of plant patents are the same with those of utility patent discussed above (there are few exceptions). Your application, as required by law, should describe the characteristics of the plant that make them unique from other known and related plants. You must also provide a comprehensive botanical description of the plant. You will find a detailed guideline on the content and arrangement of your application from Title 37 of the Code of Federal Regulations, Section 1.163(a). Below are some important details of your application and their arrangement as stipulated by the USPTO regulations.

a. Title of the invention which may include the applicant's name, residence and country of citizenship
b. Cross reference to the related applications if any
c. Statement regarding federally-sponsored research and development if there is any
d. The claimed species and genus Latin name
e. Different names of the plant
f. Background of the invention, which should describe the field of invention and relevant prior art including the information contained in 37 CFR 1.97 and 1.98.
g. Overview of the invention, which should show the main distinguishing features of the plant
h. A short description of the drawing
i. A comprehensive botanical description of the plant
j. Your claim
k. The abstract of the Disclosure (here, you are required to briefly describe the plant highlighting its essential and new characteristics)

When preparing and filing your applications, there are a number of factors that you should take into consideration.

1. Use a unique name (one not used before or that cannot be confused with any other one) for your plant. The Plant Variety Database of the International Union for the Protection of New Varieties of Plants (UPOV) will be useful to you. You have to search their old catalogue. Find more information about this union from www.upov.int. There are

other relevant international register listings that you can check before naming your new plant.

2. Support your applications with drawings. But use duplicate copies rather than the original copies. The drawing should look like the real plant, especially in colour. Your drawing should be clear and well scaled so that it can easily be reproduced.

3. Use a separate envelope to lodge each application ensuring that each envelope contains all the required documents.

4. Ensure that your application complies with the required format and content. Use already accepted applications for patent right of a plant that has some similarities with yours.

5. Make sure that your declaration or oath is one required for a plant patent application. Don't forget to sign your oath not more than three months before the date you lodge your application.

6. Use a current and correct mailing address.

7. Pay all the required fees such as filing fee, examination fee, search fee and others at the time you are lodging your application if you don't want to experience any delay in the processing of your application.

8. Include your current telephone number on your application and you can be called for pre-examination questions.

Transfer of Patents

Patent, just like other types of intellectual property, can be assigned or transferred to another person or a business to manage for them. There are a number of factors that can give rise to the transfer of a patent. Some of these factors include a merger/demerger, assignment, merger, operation of law the law, bankruptcy, operation of law etc. In the United States' Patent Act, a patent is considered to be a personal property. Consequently, it can also be transferred to another person to manage for the inventor just as one can transfer or assign their personal properties to another person to manage for them. The regulations and requirements for patent transfers and assignment in the United States of America are enshrined in Title 35 U.S.C. section 261.

According to the patent Act, there are two basic ways through which ownership of a patent can change. First, the original owner can transfer it to another person, party or entity through an assignment. Another means through which an initial patent can be altered is through a change of its name. In this case, the original owner of the patent retains ownership but changes their name. It is also possible to take a loan using a patent as a collateral. In this regard, there will be a security agreement in which the patent owner and the lender will concur that the borrower will forfeit their patent to the lender if the borrower defaults in the repayment of their loan. The US Patent Act requires that the security agreement be registered with the United States Patent and Trademark Office.

All you need to do is to negotiate terms with the entity or party that you will be assigning the patent to. When you have agreed and finalised the deal with the person and completed all the necessary documentation and paperwork, you are required to record the transfer or change of name with the USPTO. The office runs an electronic patent assignment system normally abbreviated as EPAS. Access the system online through the USPTO's website and then complete the form on the system, upload all the supporting legal documents and paperwork which must be in PDF or TIFF format. This is what is known as Patent Assignment Recordation Coversheet. If you have any questions to ask or any inquiry to make about the filing of electronic patent assignments, you have to email it to EPAS@uspto.gov.

All the recorded Patent Assignment data starting from 1980 to date are in the database of the USPTO. In case you want to obtain any information about the recorded patent transfer and change of name, you can search their database. Send any inquiry or question you may have about patent assignment search to

AssignmentSearch@uspto.gov. Note that recording a patent assignment with USPTO will attract a fee of $40 (£28.63).

When you are negotiating the transfer of your patent, you may consider hiring the services of an attorney to stand for you and negotiate the best deal for you. Also bear in mind that you are free to decide what to transfer and what to retain. Some inventors transfer some part of their patent and make money by earning royalty.

As already mentioned above, try to use an attorney or an experienced agent to help you with the negotiation. Also try to find out what the entity that you are selling your patent to will be doing with it or whether it will be developed, made and properly commercialised. There are some people that acquire a patent and leave the patented idea to remain that way so that they will be able to sell their own product and make money from the sales. It may be difficult to find out if a purchaser has such a plan in mind. The best way to avoid this is to include clauses in the transfer agreement that will prevent the purchaser from dumping your patented idea.

Jointly Owned Patent

The USPTO allows two or more people to own a patent of any type insofar as they have an agreement to do so. It is normal for two or more people who collaborated in a research to benefit from their work together. However, such a collaboration and jointly owned patent requires a well-defined agreement on the right of each of the owners to avoid any complications which may even result in court cases. The United States Patent Act has a regulation that governs jointly owned patents in cases where there is no agreement. The code that deals with joint patents is Title 35 USC 262. According to this section of the US patent law, when there is no agreement, each of the party in a joint patent has the right to use, sell, make, produce or import a patented invention without the approval of the other joint owners. An addition has been made to the stipulation of this law by a case law, which gives each of the joint owners the right to license the invention without the permission of the other owners. With these judicial pronouncements, there is nothing like the grant of an exclusive license in a jointly owned patent, unless there is a unanimous agreement of all the joint owners to utilise, produce, sell or make the invention by themselves or not to issue any further licenses.

Based on this case law, a co-owner has the right to willingly refuse to join in a suit against an infringer and his exercise of this right will prevent the others from filing a litigation against an alleged infringer. A voluntary refusal to join in a suit will give rise to a de-facto grant of a license even without a positive action. In this context, if a co-inventor has not given his or her rights to another person, he is taken to be co-owner of the entire patent. Some states such as Texas and California have community property laws. In these states, inventions made during marriage and patent granted to the inventor belongs to the couple, even if the invention is made by one of the partners. If an inventor is bound by such legislation, it is recommendable that the inventor agrees with the non-inventing spouse that the patent will not be taken as a community property. They can also have an understanding about any transfer of rights that may occur.

The US Patent law does not allow inventors to divide ownership between different claims because the patent granted belongs to the whole co-ownership. The extent of contribution made by each of the parties is not relevant here. In this regard, if only an aspect or more of the invention are jointly invented and the remaining are invented by one of the joint owners, the patent belongs to the whole party unless where there is an agreement stating the contrary.

In the employer-employee relationship, employers may not lay claim over the invention or patent of their employees unless there is an agreement mandating the employee to transfer his or her patent to the employer. This is because the general rule of patent ownership in the United States gives the patent right to the inventor. This explains why the majority of the US companies will have their employees sign an agreement that they will give their patents and other intellectual property to their employers insofar as the rights are granted when they are employed by their businesses.

Bear in mind that the parties going in to joint ownership can reach an agreement on how they would want their ownership of patent to be. They can choose to follow the general rules. They can also decide to define the right of each of the party over any of their inventions.

If you are planning to reach a joint ownership agreement with another person or group of people, it is important that you know the implication of such a collaboration, as mentioned above. This will help you to make an informed decision about the joint ownership agreement. Ensure that the terms of the patent are in your favour. Also seek for professional advice when you are going into a joint ownership of patent. A professional will be able to offer you a sound advice.

Given the implications and the ugly side of joint ownership of patents mentioned above, before you enter into joint ownership, it is advisable for you to have a thorough understanding of joint ownership in order to determine whether it is the right choice for you. If you are opting for that, you should anticipate and get ready for the possible negative outcome of joint ownership and plan measures of dealing with them or preventing their occurrence. Make sure that your interest is protected and that the rights of other joint owners do not come against or constitute an obstruction to your own right. Always negotiate for a fair share of what will come out of the partnership. One of the things that you should include in the agreement is the enforcement of the patent against an infringer or infringers as the case may be. Jointly owned patent left to the extant rules is most likely going to have a bitter ending especially when it comes to the enforcement of the patent against an infringer. So, ensure that all the points mentioned above are taken into consideration in your joint patent agreement. As advice and a warning, don't enter into a joint patent deal without having a solid agreement. You are most likely going to require the services of an attorney.

Patent Application from Foreign Nationals

The US Patent Act also covers inventions made outside the United States of America as well as inventions made by non-US citizens inside the United States of America. But each of these has its own requirements and regulations. The first point to bear in mind regarding patenting an invention made overseas or outside of the US is that a patent is territorial and thus a patent granted by the USPTO is only enforceable in the US and not outside of the US. Similarly, you cannot enforce a patent granted in other countries inside the US.

As already mentioned above, each country has its unique patent regulations. US companies existing outside of the US can protect their inventions in the countries where the inventions where made. Most small companies existing outside of the US find it difficult to protect their invention in their host countries because of lack of knowledge of the patent regulations of their host countries. So, if you invented something outside of the US and you want to patent it in the country, it is recommendable that you hire the services of a legal firm that is knowledgeable about the patent regulation of your host country to help you create a reliable IPR protection strategy. There are other steps they should consider in order to protect their intellectual property, which are listed in the website of the USPTO and include the following:

- Working with legal counsel to develop an overall IPR protection strategy;
- Developing detailed IPR language for licensing and subcontracting contracts;

- Conducting due diligence of potential foreign partners (The U.S. Commercial Service can help, see Export.gov);
- Recording their U.S.-registered trademarks and copyrights with Customs and Border Protection; and
- Securing and registering patents, trademarks, and copyrights in key foreign markets, including defensively in countries where IPR violations are common.

If you are not sure of the office that registers intellectual property in your country of host, you may check the online directory of the World Intellectual Property Office at http://www.wipo.int/directory/en/urls.jsp. Note that the process of filing for a patent in multiple countries is regulated by the Patent Cooperation Treaty (PCT). Under the regulation of PCT, if you file for patent with the USPTO, you will be eligible to obtain protection in about 143 countries. Put differently, the Patent Cooperation Treaty makes it possible and much easier for inventors to file for a patent in many countries. You can check here to find more information on this https://www.uspto.gov/patents-getting-started/international-patent-cooperation.

If you have filed for patent protection in the United States of America for an invention made in the US, you are not allowed to file or authorise or cause any person to file for patent on the same invention in another country until after six months from the time the initial application was made.

The US Patent Act also allows a foreign inventor to apply for patent protection in the US. There is no discrimination on patent protection in the US on the basis of the applicant's nationality. However, applicants who are not citizens of the US are required to satisfy certain requirements for their patent application to be processed. Below are these requirements.

The law requires foreign applicants to sign a document that shows their full name and their country of nationality. The document should also show that the original inventor is the same with the person making the declaration or the oath. The application should properly be identified by the document. Furthermore, the applicant is required to show in the document that they have read and understood the application's content. The declarant or the person making the oath is obliged to provide the USPTO with all the information about the material to be protected by the patent which the person is aware of. Consequent upon the last requirement, an information disclosure statement (IDS) is required of a foreign application. This statement should contain the prior art, which in the applicant's judgment is closer to their invention.

Completing this aspect of the legal requirements for the application of a patent is not very complicated, even though it appears to be a complex process. Though there is nothing wrong with hiring an IP attorney, you will still be able to accomplish it by yourself if you are good with paperwork. The boilerplate form (PTO/SB/01) provided by the US Patent and Trademark Office will be helpful too. It is prepared to help applicants complete the form properly.

In place of a declaration, the application can also make an oath. Many experts do not recommend the deposition of an oath because of its complex nature. Besides, the applicant will be required to depose the oath before a US diplomatic or consular officer.

Representation

Applicants who are citizens of other countries are also allowed by the US Patent to seek for legal representation or to hire an agent to represent them. However, not all legal firms, attorneys and agents are qualified to play this role. As already mentioned above, you can hire attorneys or agents registered and approved by the USPTO. Check the list of registered patent agents in the link given above to make a choice.

If you have already patented your invention abroad or have already applied for a patent abroad for over twelve months before filing your application for patent protection, your patent application will not be granted. This duration of twelve months is reduced by half if what you have applied for is a design patent. So, to be able to secure a patent protection like the US citizens, foreign applicants who have already applied for patent right protection abroad and which to secure the US patent protection should endeavour to lodge their applications within the timeframe required by law.

The above requirement is legally known as the right of priority. The 35 U.S.C 119(b) requires an applicant to claim priority of this initial application lodged in a foreign country. To secure this right, the applicant is required to provide a copy of the application filed abroad and it has to be certified by the country's patent office. You should also find out from your country of origin or the country where you have already filed for a patent protection on the same invention whether or not a foreign filing license will be required of you. If you are not sure of the best thing to do, you should contact the customer care unit of the patent unit of your country to find out what is required of you before you will be able to file for a patent in your country and in the US. When you have satisfied all the requirements for filing a foreign patent, you can now continue with the rest of the process as explained above.

Section 3: Patenting a Product in the UK

The United Kingdom has her patent laws and regulations, which spell out the requirements for the application of patent in the country. If you are seeking to apply for patent protection in the country, whether you are a UK citizen or a non-citizen, you need to find out what the law requires of you. You will find out about the patent law of the country from the UK Patents Act of 1977 as Amended. In this section, I am going to throw more light on the UK patent legislation. What to do in order to acquire a patent, how to determine whether your items are patentable and other practical issues concerning the UK patent legislation will be examined in this section, which has only one chapter.

Chapter Four: General Information about Patent Rights in the UK

As mentioned above, the United Kingdom has her unique patent laws as well as the process of applying for a patent. In this chapter, I am going to examine the patent laws of the United Kingdom to enable you to have at least a basic knowledge of the criterion for the grant of a patent in the country. You will also learn which office has the responsibility of granting patent rights. At the end of this chapter, you will also be able to gain insight into the UK laws. Keep reading to learn more.

The United Kingdom's Patent Office: Locations and Functions

As a full sovereign nation, the UK runs a unique constitution with a unique system of patent laws, even though there may be certain similarities between them and other legal systems. One of the major differences between the UK Patent System and the United States' patent system is that in the UK, inventors can seek for protection directly from the UK Intellectual Property office or apply for it at the European Patent Office if you prefer filing for it under the European Patent Convention from which the United Kingdom's Patent Act is drawn. Note that the UK has pulled out from the European Union through a national referendum. Thus, the practice of patent may be affected. There may be changes, especially for the UK inventors that prefer seeking for a European Patent Convention.

If you are filing for your patent protection under the EPC and the Patent Cooperation Treaty, you have to lodge your application through the office IPO, which is an executive agency of the Department for Business, Innovation and Skills (BIS). The 2007 Patent Rules laid down the procedures for the application.

IPO handles issues related to patents, designs and trademarks in the United Kingdom. It is the responsibility of the office to accept and assess patent applications and grant patent rights to all applicants that meet the requirements. IPO also has the responsibility of rejecting patent applications that do not meet the stipulated requirements for the issuance of patents. Apart from granting patents, IPO also maintains registers of patents and other intellectual property such as trademarks and designs.

The UK has been protecting intellectual properties of various kinds and issuing patents to encourage inventors and secure their exclusive rights over their invention for at least a stipulated period of time since the medieval time. The patent law of the country has undergone several changes since she started her patent protection regulations. The current Patent Office of the UK was established on 1 October 1852 by the Patents Law Amendment Act 1852. The sole responsibility of this office at the initial time is to handle the administration of the patent law in the UK. But as time went on, it gradually enlarged its roles discharging functions such as patent registrations of trademarks, design and copyright regulation. The assumption of more responsibilities resulted in a change of name. Today, the patent office is known as Intellectual Property Office.

The IPO is a large agency with various units discharging the rules of the agency. However, all these units come under the leadership of the Comptroller General of Patents, Designs and Trademarks who serves as the Chief Executive of IPO and the registrars of trademarks and designs.

The IPO deals with patents but it shares some of its responsibilities regarding copyright and plant breeders' rights respectively with the Department of Culture, Media and Sport and the Plant Variety Rights Office, which is an arm of the Department for Environment, Food and Rural Affairs.

Contrary to what is obtainable in the United States of America, the IPO is empowered by the Patents Act 2004 to offer non-binding suggestions and opinions on cases of patent infringement and validity to aggrieved parties. This makes it possible for them to resolve such cases without going through the expensive and complicated legal process.

The UK Patent Office is currently based in Newport, South East Wales after it was moved from Southampton Buildings, London WC2 in 1991. It still has a branch in London to serve the large number of inventors and professionals in the Capital City of England.

Visit https://www.gov.uk/government/organisations/intellectual-property-office to get contact details of the UK Patent Office and also to obtain other useful information about the office.

Types of Exclusive Rights Granted by the UK Patent Law

Quite unlike the US Patent Laws, the UK patent laws protect only inventors of machines, processes, various kinds of articles and nonobvious new improvements on them. But the UK IP laws include separate exclusive rights for the inventors of design and plant breeders. In other words, there are three classifications of exclusive rights granted to inventors by the UK IP laws if they meet the requirements. However, these rights are treated in the UK intellectual property laws as separate and distinct rights. Each has a similar meaning with the US definition of these rights. Having exhaustively looked into various kinds of patents in the several chapters above, I will only give a brief description of these rights as they are understood in the UK laws.

Patent of Invention/Utility Patent

The UK Intellectual Property Office grants inventors the protection against unauthorised use, making, marketing and selling of their ideas, inventions, processes and methods. This is what is known as patent of invention or utility patent. This is the most common. In fact, it is synonymous with patent itself. The UK government website does not treat design and plant rights as parts of patents, instead, they are treated as different kinds of rights. So, when the UK law talks of a patent, it is basically referring to the patent of utility. As already mentioned above, this right is only enforceable within the UK. This means that a patent granted by the United Kingdom's Intellectual Property Office can only be enforced within the country and not in another sovereign nation.

A product, process, method or an idea has to meet certain requirements for it to be patentable. In other words, not every article or idea is patentable under a patent of invention. If you are planning to apply for this type of patent, you should ensure that your invention satisfies the following requirements:

- Your invention must be producible and usable. The implication of this is that for an invention to be patentable, it has to be capable of industrial application. This criterion requires an invention to assume the practical form of a device, product or an apparatus like a new method of operation, industrial processes or a new material.
- The invention should be the first of its kind, meaning that it is completely new and has not been discovered and made known to the public by any person before the date of the application of patent right protection. Consequently, confidentiality is of essence here. It is highly important that you keep your invention secret if you have not filed for patent protection at the UK Intellectual Property Office. If it is necessary that you disclose it to any person, have the person sign a confidential agreement before you can disclose or discuss your invention with them. Note that if you are dealing with a patent attorney, a professional advisor or a staff member of IPO, there is no need to have the person sign the confidentiality agreement. This is because the nature of their offices demands confidentiality and they are obliged to

keep it and not to abuse the confidence reposed on them by their clients.

- An invention must involve some inventive step. In the light of this criterion, one cannot lay claim to and seek for patent protection over a simple modification made on something in existence already. This is similar to what the US Patent Law refers to as nonobvious. For a modification on an existing invention to be considered patentable, it must not be obvious to a professional or person with some level of knowledge and experience in the area when it is juxtaposed with what is already in existence.

Inventions that are not patentable

Not every invention can be protected with a patent right. As listed in the UK government website, the following kinds of inventions are not patentable:

- literary, dramatic, musical or artistic works
- a way of doing business, playing a game or thinking
- a method of medical treatment or diagnosis
- a discovery, scientific theory or mathematical method
- the way information is presented
- some computer programs or mobile apps
- 'essentially biological' processes like crossing-breeding plants, and plant or animal varieties

Check https://www.gov.uk/patent-your-invention for more information on this.

The application process

The application process for a patent in the UK is a complex one and may require expert handling. It is not advisable that you handle it by yourself. According to the UK government website, if 20 people apply for a patent without professional help, only 5% of them will be successful in their application. So, if you're planning to apply for a patent, you should seek for professional help. If you don't have the money to hire a patent attorney, you will still be able to get free patent advice. Here are the various ways of getting free patent advice:

1. Contacting a patent attorney and or a professional advisor. There are a lot of patent attorneys and professional advisors that offer a few minutes of consultation without any charge. Visit www.cipa.org.uk/find-a-patent-attorney/ for a list of reliable patent professionals.

2. British Library Business and IP Centre in London can be of help to you. You can go there to learn more about the application process for a patent in the UK. The centre is located at St Pancras, London. It is established to offer professional help to inventors and entrepreneurs. Visit their website https://www.bl.uk/business-and-ip-centre to learn more about them.

3. You should also consider attending an intellectual property clinic to broaden your knowledge about intellectual properties, including patents. The centres where the workshops are organised are spread across the country. There are centres in most major cities in the UK. Check https://www.gov.uk/government/publications/uk-patlib-network/uk-patlib-contact-information to find out where the centres are located.

Another important point you should take note of is that the patent application process in the UK is quite costly and time consuming. It will take about 5 years for an application to be processed because of the various stages involved. The entire process, including the patent attorney fee, may cost you about 4,000GBP. The UK patent is renewed on a yearly basis until it expires after 20 years. Visit https://www.gov.uk/renew-patent to know more about the renewal cost and when to renew it.

Essential parts of patent application

If you have made up your mind to apply for a patent, you should ensure that your application is complete with all the essential parts. A good patent application should have four basic parts, which include the following:

a. A good patent application should include a description of the invention to enable others to understand how the invention can be put into use and how it can be produced.

b. Your application should also contain your claim, which defines the unique technical features of the invention that you want to protect.

c. Your application must contain an abstract, which summarises the important technical aspects of your inventions.

d. The last important part of any patent application is the drawing of the invention.

It is not enough to provide all these basic parts. You have to ensure that they all satisfy their specific criteria. The instructions and manner in which they are supposed to be produced are stipulated in patent application fact sheets. You will find them at https://www.gov.uk/government/publications/patent-fact-sheets. IPO accepts applications without the claims and abstract. But they have to be submitted afterwards otherwise the application will not be successful. Experts recommend the submission of a complete package, that is, an application with all its parts.

Certain applicants are required to provide a statement of inventorship. Applications made on behalf of a company, not made by the inventor and applications which do not contain a list of all the inventors (in the case of an invention made by more than one person) are those that should include a statement of inventorship. The statement of inventorship form can be completed online and submitted when filing an application. It can also be downloaded and submitted along the line with the application. You can also submit your application first and then submit your statement of inventorship afterwards. IPO also accepts academic papers that describe an invention but they cannot serve as substitutes for the description and drawing of your invention. They only help to make the description clearer.

A patent application package can be sent to IPO via post. You can also create the application online. The fees for each of these types of application methods are not the same. For example, the online application fee is 20GBP while application by post attracts a fee of 30GBP. Apart from the application fee, the applicants are also required to pay the search and substantive examination fees, which respectively cost 130GBP and 80GBP for the online application and 150GBP and 100GBP for applications lodged via the post. In all, you will spend a total of 230GBP for the online application and 280GBP for the offline application.

To facilitate the processing of your patent application, it is advisable that you file and pay for search and examination requests at the same time with your application. However, there are conditions that may result in a quick procession of a patent. Find out more about the conditions for accelerated procedures at https://www.gov.uk/government/publications/patents-fast-grant.

You can also apply for the patent search and substantive examination afterwards. But if you are applying for it afterwards, the request has to be made within 12 months from your priority date or the time you made the application. The same thing applies to the substantive examination except that the request has to be made within 6 months of the publication.

The reason for the patent search is to ensure that your invention satisfies the criterion of novelty and inventiveness. IPO will send you a copy of the search result when they are through. It will take up to 6 months for the search to be completed. Once the search is completed and all necessary documents submitted, the application will be publicised. The law requires that it be published 18 months from the time the application is lodged or from the priority date. IPO will post the open part of the application on its website for public access. It is also kept on IPO records.

After the search has been carried out on your invention, the next thing to be done is the substantive examination. The aim of the substantive check is to find out whether the claimed invention is really novel and inventive. Through this search, IPO will also find out whether your claim and descriptions are the same and meet the requirements for a patent. IPO will inform you of their findings. If your invention is not patentable or does not satisfy all the requirements, they will also let you know.

The substantive examination takes time to be completed. You may have to wait for a number of years before the process is completed. There are different ways of applying for it. You can request for that via the Internet. In an online application, IPO allows applicants to send their substantive examination request together with their online application. They can also apply for it after they might have lodged their application but that has to be done within the stipulated time period. Visit https://www.gov.uk/apply-for-a-patent.

Once you have successfully completed your application, paid all the necessary fees and request for search and substantive examination, IPO will issue you with a receipt showing the date the application is filed and your application number. IPO will inform you of what is next to be done. If a positive decision is taken on your application, you will be issued with a certificate and the final form of your application is published. During the period when your application is still pending, you need to mark it pending or patent applied for.

Withdrawal of Application

IPO allows applicants to withdraw their application in case they don't want it to be publicised any more. However, the withdrawal has to be done before it is published. The search report will indicate the deadline for withdrawal of application in case you want to do so. You can send your withdrawal request through the post or email or by fax. The withdrawal request should show your application number and why you are the rightful person to apply for the withdrawal (for example, you are the applicant or the agent to the inventor). If you are withdrawing via email, send your request to withdraw@ipo.gov.uk. For fax, send it to 01633817777. If you prefer sending it via post, address your withdrawal request to:

Intellectual Property Office
Concept House
Cardiff Road
Newport
South Wales
NP10 8QQ
United Kingdom.

IPO also allows withdrawal of applications for the purposes of reapplication afterwards. So, in case you want to amend your application or certain things are not right with it, you can withdraw it, get it right, include all the necessary information and then reapply after you are ok with that. If the initial application is not yet up to a year from the time you made it, you can use the date it was filed for the new application. This is what is known as the priority date.

Note that IPO processes only complete applications with all the necessary documentations. All fees have to be paid. If you didn't meet the requirement and payment, your application will be terminated after a period of twelve months. But you can also reapply within a year from the date your initial application was terminated. However, you will be required to pay a non-refundable application fee of 150GBP. Your applications should include reasons why you were not able to meet the requirements of the initial application and that the failure is not voluntary. Also mention when you will be able to satisfy all the requirements. The request for the resubmission of the application may be rejected or accepted. But if it is accepted, you have only two months to meet all its requirements. If your request is rejected and you feel like the rejection is unjust or unfair, you can file for ex parte hearing.

Design Protection

The UK Intellectual Property Office grants another type of protection called design protection or design right. This right as mentioned above does not come under the patent law of the UK. It is regarded as a separate right. But the USPTO regards it as a type of patent. In the UK, the right is granted in order to protect the shape, appearance or configuration of an object or a material. Just as it is the case in the US, you can apply for both the patent of utility and design patent if you meet the requirements.

Getting the design right or registering your design is not a simple process that you can easily carry out by yourself. You may also require expert advice. So, meet with an expert to learn more about this type of right, how to protect it and the requirements for securing it. You can also enforce your design right and initiate a legal action against an infringer. This again will require professional advice.

The design right is issued to exclude or stop others from using, copying, recreating or reproducing a design for a period of about 25 years. However, a design must meet certain requirements before an exclusive right is granted to the creator. But during this period, the holder of the right is required by law to renew the right after every 5 years with some fees. The first thing that you should be aware of is that the design right protects only the appearance, physical shape, decoration and configuration of an article, which refers to the manner in which the various components of the items are arranged.

If you are issued with a design right, you have an exclusive right over the design. With that right, you can also go to court against any person infringing on the right by copying, using or recreating your design without your express permission.

Just like the patent protection, not every design qualifies for the design right. You can only register your design if it is:

- novel
- not an invention or not about the mechanism or functionality of a product
- your own design
- not offensive (like containing graphic images and words)

Your design should also not utilise protected emblems or flags such as The Royal Crown, National Emblems, Olympic Rings and the likes, otherwise it will not be registered.

Though the design of a product is strongly attached to its functions, the design right does not protect the functionality of a product. This comes under the domain of the patent protection right. The UK design registration law requires a design inventor to have a clear illustration of their designs before applying for its registration. The illustration should make use of photographs, line drawings and computer-aided design (CAD) to show the design as it will appear to the naked eye.

It should contain all the details of the design in a plain background without showing any measurements as well as technical information. Whatever you use in illustrating the design, whether it is a photo or line drawing, it should be the same all through and not a combination of both. To register the surface pattern of a design, the illustration must show the entire pattern and how it repeats.

You can apply for your design registration via the post or through the Internet. The illustration for the online registration of design must be up to 8 with each file showing one view. On the contrary, if you are applying via post, you have to include over 12 illustrations with each appearing on plain A4 paper. Applicants are allowed to provide additional relevant information or details when they want to register the shape as well as a part of their illustrations. This does not include colour and surface pattern.

There are two major ways of registering a part of illustration. They include limitation and disclaimer. The former is when you explain or show only the parts of illustration to be registered. While the latter is when you show or explain the parts that you don't want to register. Each of these can be accomplished in three major ways. The first one is by circling the parts in question. The second is to grey them out. The third way of doing this is to include a line of text.

Design registration is done free of charge. You pay some money but the more designs you register, the lower the amount you will pay. For example, it will cost you 50GBP to register just one design while you will spend only $70 (£50.11) if you register up to 10 designs at the same time. Check https://www.gov.uk/register-a-design/apply to know more about the application fees. Note that it is more expensive to apply through the post than to apply online. A complete application package for design registration should include the fee sheet, the illustration itself and the application form. Download the application   from https://www.gov.uk/government/publications/application-to-register-one-or-more-design.

It takes about two weeks for an application to be accessed and registered by the Intellectual Property Office. However, there may be an objection against your application. If there are any objections, you will be given a two-month grace to respond to it. A registered design will be publicised and will remain effective for five years. In case your application is refused and you are not happy with the refusal or the decision taken, you can request for a hearing, which is of various kinds, such as an exparte hearing, joint hearing and the likes. Check https://www.gov.uk/guidance/designs-disputes-resolution-hearings for details about design dispute resolution hearings. Note that IPO does not charge any fee for a hearing but the process and the outcome may give rise to some expenses.

You can also defer the registration of your design. But the deferral has to be made within 12 months. If you fail to meet the 12 month deadline, your application will be cancelled and you will start afresh when you are ready to continue.

Plant Breeder's Right

The USPTO grants plant patents but there is nothing like a plant patent in the United Kingdom. Instead, a separate type of right is given to plant breeders in the UK. This is called the plant breeders' rights. It is issued to plant breeders that discovered, developed and bred a new plant variety or if such a breeder chooses you as their successor. For a plant breeder to be issued with this right, the person must have a plant variety that is unique in its characteristics. The repeated propagation of the variety is also required to produce plants with the same characteristics.

Plant developed under a work-for-hire agreement cannot be registered as the right belongs to the employer and not the employee. Plants that have been used for commercial purposes or that have been sold within the United Kingdom for over a year are not eligible to be protected with this right. This thing applies to plants that have been used or sold within the European Union for over 4 years before the filing of the application (the deadline for trees and vines in this regard is 6 years).

Any plant breeder that receives this right has an exclusive right to produce, reproduce, export, sell, modify for propagation purposes and keep stock of their plant varieties. Plant breeders' rights last for 25 years except trees, vine and potato varieties, which last for 30 years. Visit https://www.gov.uk/guidance/plant-breeders-rights#who-can-apply to learn more about the registration process, naming of a plant, the fees and other important information about the plant breeders' right. You can file your application via email or post. For email application use NLPBR-Applications@apha.gsi.gov.uk. If you are sending it by post, use this address:

Plant Variety Right Office
Animal and Plant Health Agency
Eastbrook
Shaftesbury Road
Cambridge
CB2 8DR
United Kingdom.

In case you have any inquiries or question to ask, kindly send an email to pvs.helpdesk@apha.gsi.gov.uk.

The Nature of the Patent Right Granted

Patent is considered to be a contract between the state and an individual or a business that invented a product, method or process. In this contract, the state grants an individual an exclusive right and monopoly over their invention in an exchange for the disclosure of the invention to the public. In light of the above, an invention that is already publicised before the patent application cannot be protected by the patent right.

Secondly, in the UK, the right granted by the state to an inventor for disclosing an invention to the public does not offer the inventor the right to execute or put their invention into use. Instead, it stops other people from using, making, importing or exporting your invention without your authority. For example, if you invent a new ticketing system for a particular type of transport system and you protect it with a patent, you don't have the right to produce cars using the ticketing system if another person has initially patented the basic invention of a car.

A patent as a kind of protection is quite territorial. Consequently, a patent granted by the UK Intellectual Property Office does not offer you any protection in other countries of the world. The right is only respected within the United Kingdom, as already explained. In case you want a patent protection in multiple countries, take a look again at what has been said above on how to obtain patent protection in more than one country.

The Article 69 EPC determines the scope of patent protection in the UK. According to this Article, what determines the scope of a patent protection is the language of the claims which are interpreted with the description and drawings included in the illustration. However, the Protocol on the Interpretation of Article 69 of the EPC made it clear that this interpretation should go beyond the literal meaning of the wording used in the claims, drawings and description. Additionally, the Article of the Protocol also says "But Article 69 should also not be understood as saying that the claims serve only as a guideline and that the actual protection conferred may extend to what, from considering the description and drawings, the patentee may have more widely contemplated as their invention. Instead, claims must be interpreted as defining a position between these two extremes which combines a fair protection for the patentee with a reasonable degree of certainty for third parties." The application of the above is that it is wrong to interpret the scope of a patent protection issued by IPO based on these two extremes.

Article 2 was added in the 2000 revision by EPC in order to deal with the issue of the scope of the patent. According to this Article "…for the purpose of determining the extent of protection conferred by a European patent, due account shall be taken of any element which is equivalent to an element specified in the claims."

In recent times, the UK Supreme Court, in the Acavis vs. Eli Lilly case, extended the scope of the UK patent protection beyond the claims to include variants, which in a substantially similar manner, produce results that are substantially the same with the patented invention in question. However, in arriving at this conclusion, the Supreme Court also added that it has to be obvious to a person skilled in the art that the variant substantially yields the same effect with the patented invention in a way that is substantially the same with what has been patented.

Using Another's Patent Rights

Just as with some other types of intellectual properties, one can also transfer or give their patent rights to another person in an exchange for what a patentee considers as valuable, which in most cases is money. There are basically two major ways that one can use another person's or business' patent. The first way is to obtain a license from the person and the second way is to purchase the patent from the inventor. However, each of these options has its requirements.

The agreement or any licensing arrangement is between the patentee and the person to hold the license. IPO does not decide everything in any licensing arrangement. In fact, the bulk of the agreement will be made between you and the prospective license holder. IPO can only determine what should be included and what should not be included in the licence agreement. It is also left for IPO to decide whether the patentee will grant what is known as a compulsory license under a patent. But it is left for both parties to negotiate favourable terms for themselves.

If you want to obtain a licence to use a patent, it is also important that you reach a favourable agreement with the licence owner before you can use the patent. There are some patents that have what is known as license of right. Licence of right means that the license owner is willing to grant a licence to any interested part. Such willingness does not mean that you should not negotiate favourable terms for yourself. It is recommended that you meet with a professional or patent attorney to negotiate favourable terms for you. IPO may also help you out if there is no favourable agreement with the patentee.

When you have issued another person the license to use your patent, you should also register it with IPO. The registration process is quite simple. It is as simple as completing the Patent Form 21. The form is available   at https://www.gov.uk/government/publications/application-to-register-or-give-notice-of-rights. The form contains the address where you should post it to. If you have multiple licences for different licences, you will also be able to record them on the form. However, you will be charged 50GBP for each form you submit.

Purchasing a patent

A patent can also be sold by one patentee to another. However, the patentee is required by law to transfer ownership to the new owner or the person that purchases the patent. The transfer is recorded in a written document to be signed by the seller of the patent. The written document is called an assignment. You may hire a solicitor or patent law firm to draw up the assignment for you. A copy of the assignment should be sent together with patents form 21 to the address contained on the form. Multiple licences for different patents can be recorded in the form. But bear in mind that you will be charged 50GBP for each form you send.

Jointly Owned Patent

It is not uncommon for two individuals or businesses to partner together in researching and developing a product, method or process. Such partnership requires the parties involved to reach certain agreements with each other. One of the important matters to agree on before beginning the project is the patent ownership. It is important to arrive at such an agreement. This is because the UK has her law and regulations regarding ownership of patents in such a collaborative effort. If you are going into such an agreement, you should know what your rights are and their limits as well as the rights of your partners and their limits. There are different ways through which ownership can be allocated and each of these approaches has its own pros and cons. It is therefore pertinent that you enter into such a deal with caution and ensure that you go for an option that suits you the most.

It can be quite challenging to allocate patent ownership of jointly owned inventions. This is because the nature of the invention or the outcome of the project that will result in the invention is not yet clear at the beginning. Besides, at this time, the future value of the patented invention is still not known. Another reason why the allocation of a jointly owned patent can be difficult is that each of the parties involved in the partnership may have different objectives and agendas, which may at times conflict with each other.

Sometimes, people collaborate to make an invention thinking that the patent will be equally owned or according to the contribution made by each person. But it is always good to take into consideration what the patent law says. The stipulations of the patent law may sometimes have some unsavoury consequences that may result in fruitless litigations. Recall that the US patent law allows each party in a joint patent ownership to use, sell, produce or export the invention with or without the consent of the other parties involved in the deal, unless when there is a contrary agreement.

Similarly, the UK Patent Law, as contained in section 36 (1) of the manual of patent practice, states that "where a patent is granted to two or more people, each of them shall, subject to any agreement to the contrary, be entitled to an equal undivided share in the patent. The paragraph 2 of the same section further gives each of the parties (or their agents) the right to use the patented invention as they deem fit without the consent of the other co-owner(s) unless if there is a contrary agreement. The UK patent law on joint ownership is quite similar to that of the US. Consequent upon that, it is easy for disputes and disagreements to ensue, especially when the extent of ownership is not well defined in a well prepared and signed document, regardless of the manner in which the ownership is allocated.

As already mentioned, the best way to avoid a dispute over a jointly owned patent is to define on time how the patent should be allocated. Nowadays, there are ways of allocating a patent in a joint inventive venture or project as explained below.

Ways of Allocating Patent for Jointly Owned Invention
If you are collaborating with a person or a business to invent something, here are various approaches of allocating a patent in a successful project.

Ownership based on inventorship
In this type of arrangement, ownership of patent is given to any of the parties that discovers or makes the invention. If the invention is made by two people or businesses, the patent belongs to the two of them. If this approach appeals to you, it will also be good that you decide on how the patent owners should use them, especially if the discovery is made by two people or more people. The major problem with this type of patent allocation is defining or determining who makes an invention, as it is possible for every party to lay claim to it.

Allocation of ownership based on the subject matter

A patent can also be allocated based on its subject matter, regardless of who makes the invention or whether it relates solely to the background technology of one of the party. This arrangement works well in a joint venture agreement in which each of the parties involved in the partnership has a discreet portfolio or in a situation where the respective fields of the parties are well defined.

Combined approach

The two approaches discussed above can be combined in the allocation of a patent. The parties may agree that the patent belongs to the person or business that makes the invention insofar as it is not in the same subject matter or background technology of the other party (s) involved in the partnership. They can also agree that a patent will be allocated based on subject matter and when it does not fall within the defined field, the person that makes the invention will own the patent.

Note that none of these approaches is trouble-free. Disputes, which may escalate to court cases, may arise with each of them. So, it is always good to develop strategies and plan on how to avoid disputes or deal with them when they arise in the future as a result of joint ownership.

International Patents

As explained above, a patent is territorial. It can only be enforced in a country where it is granted. But if you want a wider protection of invention, you should file a single application under the Patent Cooperation Treaty (PCT). Visit www.wipo.int/pct/en/ to learn more about PCT. If you are successful with the application, you will enjoy protection in over 140 countries. If you file your application under the European Patent Office (EPO), your invention will be protected in over 30 countries in Europe.

Another means of getting multiple patent protections is to apply for a patent in different countries. Visit www.wipo.int/directory/en/urls/jsp to get the contact details of the intellectual property offices of various countries.

Section 4: Making Money from Your Ideas

In the preceding sections, I have spent time discussing patents, its meaning, benefits, usefulness, the patent rules and practices of various parts of the world especially, the US and UK, and how you will patent your ideas in these countries to help you know exactly what to do when you make an invention. But it is not enough to patent your invention and ideas. You need to also know how to make money from it. Thus, in this section, I will be discussing how you can make some money from your patented ideas and inventions. Your idea will come to nothing if you're not able to turn it into a money making machine. In the subsequent chapter of this book, I shall tell you how to market and sell an idea/invention for gain.

Chapter Five: Ways of Making Money from Your Ideas/Invention

When you have registered your ideas/invention, the next stage is to implement it in order to make money from it. If you discover or invent something, you're supposed to experience a remarkable improvement in the quality of your life because ideas are money. However, some inventors' quality of life remains the same even after making inventions. The reason for this is because they don't know how to sell their ideas. In this chapter, I am going to tell you the various ways you can make money from your idea.

Four Ways of Generating Revenue from Your Inventions

There are several ways through which you can make money from your invention. Here are the various ways of doing that.

1. Having it all done by yourself

Here, you will have to do everything by yourself. This means you will be responsible for the implementation of your idea as well as the marketing, selling and exportation of the products resulting from your idea or invention. This option is a nice option for people that have money to pay for all the stages involved in the production, marketing and selling of goods until it gets to the last consumer. The financial demand of this option may be quite much. Thus, if you are not financially strong, you may consider other options. However, if you have all it takes to implement your invention, market and sell it, you stand a very big chance of making money from your invention.

2. Collaborating with others

If you don't have the money to turn your idea into a finished product so that it can be marketed and sold to the final consumers but you want to take part in the entire process, you will still be able to implement your ideas. You can do that by partnering with other people. There are a lot of people looking for where to invest their money. Typical examples of such individuals are the angel investors. They fund start-ups, especially those with the potential of giving them high return on investment. So, if you lack funds to implement your invention, you may consider looking for such individuals to partner with.

Angel investors are good sources of raising funds to start a business or manufacture a product. The problem with this option is that you have to look for such individuals. Finding them may not be easy, especially if you don't have many connections. However, the Internet technology has made it much easier to reach a large number of angel funders. There is what is known as equity crowdfunding. This is a term used to refer to the Internet type of private investors that pull resources together in order to fund implementation of ideas and inventions. They have networks nowadays. So, join such a network online. Take time to learn about and how it works. Definitely, if you have a nice idea, they will be willing to sponsor you. In return, they will get equity, that is, they will get a share in the business. Each owns to the extent they have provided. It works like traditional stock. Consequently, it is a part of the capital markets.

Whether you are going offline or online, when negotiating the deal, ensure that you get a contract that favours you and gives you a fair share of whatever that may come out of the transaction. Remember that the fund may not be yours but the idea or invention is yours and nobody can implement it within the period of time your patent right protection allows you. So, you are the only person that has the right to implement or authorise another person to implement it for you. Armed with this knowledge, you have some edge in the negotiation process. You may require an experienced individual or a legal firm to help you with the contract. Note that any contract you sign is a legal document and a violation of it can result in court proceedings.

So, ensure that you understand every aspect of the contract before signing it.

   3.   Subcontracting the manufacturing process

The most expensive aspect of the implementation of an invention is the manufacturing aspect. Though the cost implication depends on the type and nature of ideas in question, if you don't have enough money, you will not be able to produce anything. Production of any item entails a lot of things. You will require manpower, machines and other equipment to make anything. Apart from the financial demands of production, the process is also complicated and may be difficult. Many production processes of any product require more than one person. So, if you are looking to implement your idea or invention, you should have the physical ability and strength to meet up with the demand of the process. It is also time consuming to make something. Production, starting from the time of accessing raw materials to the time when the goods are finalised, normally takes time to be completed. It requires patience, determination and courage. Even if you meet the physical and financial requirements to implement your idea or invention, you still need these virtues and internal disposition.

Your option, as many inventors do, is to contract the implementation of their invention to another company or person and then deal with the marketing and selling of the product by themselves. This option reduces your involvement with the entire process of the implementation and marketing of ideas. The advantage of this option is that it provides you the opportunity of participating at least in a stage in the implementation process of your idea.

There are also some people that may prefer to subcontract the marketing, selling and exportation of the finished product while they handle the production process by themselves. It is your choice to make. But make sure that you choose any aspect that you can handle very well.

4. Licensing your intellectual property rights to a company

The last means of making money from your invention is to give another company the license to produce, manufacture, market and sell the product made from your idea. The licensee will pay you royalty from the revenue they make from the use of your idea. The royalty depends on the agreement you have with them. It can be a lump sum or a percentage of each unit product sold. The royalty can also be paid for a stipulated number of years. So, you need to ensure that you negotiate a favourable term for yourself.

If you prefer licensing your product, make sure you keep to the licensing requirements of the relevant authority in your country. In this way, you will not have any problem with anyone.

Having explained briefly the various ways you can make money from your idea, I am going to provide you with tips on how to market and sell your idea or product made from it in the subsequent chapter.

Chapter Six: How to Market and Sell Your Idea

This is the last chapter of this section and it provides you with important tips on how to take the product made from your idea to the market and or to the final consumers.

Marketing and Selling Your Idea

If you are a salesperson or you are into marketing, you will agree with me that it is not easy to convince a consumer to purchase a finished product; even a product with known benefits. Indubitable, it will be much more difficult to market a new idea or invention because the consumers are not yet sure whether all the claims about the inventions are true or not. Your success depends on how you go about it. If you approach it with the right strategy, then you will succeed. But with a wrong strategy, you will fail. In this chapter, I am going to discuss the proven strategies that you can use to sell your newly patented invention and ideas.

Factors to Take into Consideration Before You Market an Idea

Before you start marketing and selling your ideas or inventions, there are a number of factors that you should take into consideration which include the following:

Knowing that it is not about you

In the business world of today, consumers and decision makers don't care about your feelings, difficulties and suffering. They are not interested in whatever explanation you have. They are only interested in what you can offer them. They want to know if your idea can improve or solve their problems. They are interested in things that will improve their lives and make them more comfortable. For those in business, only inventions that make their consumers happy and help them to make more sales are welcome.

So, nobody wants you to talk about your problem, how hard you work to make the invention, your sacrifices and sleepless nights. Put differently, your idea does not actually interest the decision maker but what they can gain from it or the value it will give them does. So, you should bear this fact in mind when you are preparing for your presentation. When preparing your speech, take yourself as the consumer or a decision maker and ask yourself this basic question "why should I care about this" or "of what use will this idea to my business"? The answer to this question will tell you whether you are selling value or providing solution to them or not. It is good that you are honest in answering this question. If you think that your invention is of value to them, you can continue with your preparation.

Be a good listener

There is the tendency for some people to pay much attention to their presentation and pay little attention to their audience, end users, managers and clients. But it is of crucial importance and in fact, it pays to listen to the end-users and decision makers before and during the presentation of ideas. This highlights the importance of sitting back and listening to feedback as they come. Your end-users, or the decision makers, know their business and what will be of help to them. So, listening to them will help you to improve on your idea.

Make it a business proposition

Think of your idea presentation as a type of business proposition. As such, you have to make it quite compelling, lively and convincing. Capture the attention of the audience/decision makers with stunning designs and captivating visuals. Don't forget to hit the nail on the head. It is not an academic presentation. So, make it simple and use ease-to-understand language. Your audience is there to know how your idea or invention will be of help to their business and not to listen to intelligent wording. So, use the language of their business, which they can easily understand and follow. They are not interested in your degrees. Give them a good idea that will help them to make more sales and they will follow you. The implication of this is that before you go for the presentation of an idea, you should take time to learn about the industry, the product your idea will be applied to and have a good mastery of the language of the industry.

Don't overlook the core values

As already mentioned above, you always give your listeners or audience the reason to purchase from you. A good way to ensure that you achieve that is stay focus on the core values of the business. Put differently, you should know the business or individuals you are presenting to very well. Knowing them here does not mean having any relationship with them before the presentation. It simply means that you should take time to research about the business to get some basic or background information about it. Find out who their customers are. It is also advisable that you speak with them before the presentation, as this will help you to establish some rapport with them. Besides, many experts are of the opinion that knowing the personality of the decision makers or any person you are selling to will be of help to you. For example, if you are going to pitch to a person that likes creativity and you discover that earlier, you will work hard to highlight novelty and the creative aspect of your idea and invention.

Keep it simple

As a rule of thumb, it is the best practice to go straight to the point when making your presentation. There is no need to beat about the bush or make unnecessary elaboration. Make the number of slides you are using as few as possible. However, being precise does not mean that you should overlook the important points or aspects of your presentation.

Don't overlook the weaknesses

There is no perfect idea or invention. So, when you are presenting or pitching your ideas, don't give your listeners the impression that it is a flawless invention. This is because when they start implementing your ideas, they will eventually discover the imperfections or short comings of your ideas. When they do, they will not have any trust in you again. So, when you are presenting your ideas, don't forget to mention their shortcoming at least briefly. But it is not enough to mention the negative aspects of your invention. You have to also let them know that you anticipated the drawbacks and that you are working hard to improve on that. As you are preparing your presentation, also get ready to answer why questions. "The why" questions are normally tough. Sometimes, it may be about your idea or your future plan. No matter where it comes from, the truth is that you should not allow yourself to be caught unaware. Always have plausible answers to them.

Believe in Your Idea and Yourself

To sell your idea to another person and make money from it, you have to believe in yourself and your idea otherwise you will not be able to convince others to use or buy it. Imagine a salesperson that has no belief in the products they are selling. In the same manner, if you have no belief in your creativity or you doubt it, how do you expect a decision maker to believe in it? Your creativity or ideas may be strongly criticised. But no matter how intense the criticisms are, you don't have to lose your trust in your creativity because you are good at what you do. Sometimes criticisms, especially when they are constructive, are good. They may be an opportunity for you to discover the loopholes of your invention and a better way to improve on it. Sometimes, an invention may be criticised because it is quite a brilliant idea. So, they should not make you lose your trust in your idea. Instead, learn from them.

The above are some of the helpful tips that you can apply in order to make a nice presentation of your ideas. You may find some other useful tips elsewhere. A bad presentation will have a terrible consequence. There are a lot of people out there with nice ideas and inventions but they are not able to present them very well to convince inventors to put their money there. You will definitely get investors and decision makers that will be ready to stake their money on your idea if they find it useful.

Marketing a Physical Product

As I have explained above, you can invent a physical product, a process, or a method. The way you market or sell a physical product is different from the way you sell a non-tangible product. The previous subheading concerns marketing and selling of non-tangible invention, which can be referred to as ideas. Here, I am going to provide you with tips on how to market and sell your physical product.

In the business world of today, products and services are marketed and sold online and offline. So, if you invent and make a new product, you can sell it online or offline. You can also combine the two methods to maximise profit. I am going to provide you with tips on how to market on both mediums.

Marketing and selling a newly invented product online

It can be quite challenging to market a newly invented product, as consumers are not quite sure of how they are going to benefit from it. So, you need to go the extra mile to convince them to purchase your product rather than those of your competitors, which they have been purchasing before yours. The first step to take is to ensure that your product is of good quality. Before your invention, consumers have been surviving on something. You have to give them reasons or convince them to purchase your product and not what they have before. The best reason to give them is to have something of great quality or something better than what they had before the introduction of your product. So, work out how to make a great product. When you have a great product the next task is to popularise it and make the people know about it. This is the aspect that I am going to provide you with tips on.

❖ Building your own website and blog

You need to have a website with a blog where you can talk about your business and drive traffic to it. It is your store or warehouse where consumers will come to look for your product. If you don't have a website, you are like an offline seller who does not have a store.

❖ Drive traffic to your website

Now that you have created your own website, you have to direct online traffic to your website. This entails promoting your website and driving enough online traffic to it. There are different ways of driving traffic to a website. You will get better results if you combine or apply multiple methods together. Some require more money and time than others. So, take time to study them and apply the ones that you can. You can also hire some professionals in each of the methods to help you out if you don't have the time to do them effectively. Here are ways of generating traffic to your website.

❖ On-page SEO

SEO is an acronym for search engine optimisation. It is one of the acceptable methods of increasing the visibility and ranking of a website on a search engine. Armed with a good SEO strategy, you will be able to drive traffic to your website. Today, there are several SEO strategies utilised by various online businesses and SEO professionals. One of the commonly used SEO strategies is including high-quality content with a brief meta-description on your webpages. Each meta-description tells you about a page briefly and they show on the search result below your website URL. Internet consumers will immediately find out what the page is all about when they perform a search on your keyword. It is not enough to have good content. It has to be optimised with the right keywords. If you don't have a good SEO strategy, you may consider hiring one.

❖ Article writing

Another good means of popularising a product online, whether it is a new one or an existing one, is through article writing. You can write articles on your niche and post them on your preferred online article directories. But bear in mind that some online article directories have higher credibility or are more popular than others. It will be better that you post your articles in popular article directories. Don't forget to include the link to your website in the articles. You should also include a call to action in the articles. Readers can click on your link to get to your website. Besides, including your website links in the article is very important for website ranking because the search engine recognises websites with more backlinks. In addition to posting articles on online article directories, you can also consider creating a blog where you will post your articles. Some websites have blogs.

❖ Make use of the social media with Hashtags

The social media networks such as Facebook, Instagram, Twitter and others are good mediums of creating awareness about a new product. You can increase your customer base through them. They are great platforms of getting a large customer base. These social media platforms have millions of users. This implies that any message posted there easily spreads to millions of people. So, if you utilise them very well, lots of people will come to know about your product in a couple of months. Take time to learn how each of them work. You can concentrate on one or two or even more depending your time and money. There are professional freelancers that help businesses to promote their brands and products and services through social media. You may consider hiring them if you are not able to do it yourself.

❖ Use Email Marketing

Email marketing is an effective strategy of marketing a product through the Internet. With this method, you can stay in touch with your existing customers and get new ones by sending out newsletters and promotional offers via emails. Your newsletter should include links to your landing pages and website pages for your readers to take the required action if you captivate their interest.

❖ Online advertising

Just as you can advertise your products offline, you can also do online ads. There are various ways of doing that. Joining Google advertising programs called Google Adwords will be a nice option for you. There is also social media advertising as well as display advertising, pay-per-click and paid search.

❖ Online forum

You can join and create online forums for people that have interest in your product. This is a good way of creating awareness and getting people to know about your product.

❖ Always take time to evaluate your analytics

You should incorporate tracked links into your marketing campaign strategies and ensure that you view the analytics of your website. This will help you to find out the strategies that work best for you and those that yielded better results.

The above are few of the strategies that you can use to promote your newly discovered products online. There are other ones that you can apply which are not mentioned here. Carry out further research on this to learn about others. If you put in a sincere effort in promoting your product online, you will get a lot of traffic on your website. The next thing is to choose a means of selling your product. You can create an ecommerce website through which consumers will order your product. You can also sell your product on online marketplaces and large shopping sites like Amazon and eBay. Price your product very well and reasonable. Give discounts and offer promos to attract consumers. You can also include affiliate marketing in your marketing campaign so that others will join in selling your product.

❖ Selling your product offline

You will also market and sell your product offline. This is the traditional method of selling items. So, you need to also use the traditional methods in marketing your products. Here are the various ways of marketing and advertising your product offline.

❖ Invest in mass media advertising

Mass Media advertising is a veritable means of reaching out to a large number of people at the same time. Typical examples of such means are advertising on the television, radio, magazines and newspapers. The major problem with this method of advertising is that they are very expensive. Not every business or individual can foot their bill. But if you have the money to go into them, they are very effective and will be useful to you.

❖ Billboard and banner advertising

This is also widely used traditional method of advertising. With it, you can get to thousands of people at the same time. It is not as costly as media advertising but depending on the type you're using; you may have to put in enough energy. Besides, it is difficult – if not impossible – to analyse and determine its result.

❖ Guest speaker

Look for events and ceremonies that will attract a lot of people and then see if you will be allowed to talk about your product. Some event organisers can allow you to be a guest speaker and charge you while some may not charge you, especially if your speech will benefit the audience. You can also visit universities, big companies and other places and seek for audiences with the students or staff of the businesses in question. Learn how to deliver such a speech. But in summary, you need to apply the general marketing principles.

❖ Use promotional items to get new customers and reward existing ones

Offer discounts, promos and give out free branded items to your customers. Many consumers are looking for opportunities for a good bargain. Some buy products that they don't need at the moment simply because it is sold at a good price.

❖ Organise free workshops/library sessions

A good way of speaking to people about your product is to organise free workshops and/or library sessions. Many people disregard a product because they have not been told about it or because they don't know that the product will be of help to them. Use such sessions and opportunities to explain the features of your product and how it will benefit the users and why they should purchase it rather than those of your competitors. When talking, it is not good to mention your competitors by name. So, avoid directing your criticism to any particular company or product, otherwise you may be sued for defamation.

❖ Engage in offline networking

Offline networking is nothing but coming in contact with people and connecting with them while at the same time letting them know about your product. There are different ways of achieving this. Start by establishing strong rapport with other business owners. Even though the business is competitive, you don't have to become other businesses' enemies. Join groups and offline forums. Make friends and build relationships that will be of help to you.

❖ Attend trade fairs/expos

Expos or trade fairs are great channels of selling one's products quickly. They are also avenues of building up strong relationships with other businesses and networking with others. Like-minds meet in expos. So, you will definitely find people that are interested in your product. They will help you to promote it. Consumers will also see your product as they move from one stand to another. Convince them to purchase from your stand. Even if you don't have a stand, you can also attend an expo just to meet people and make friend. In this way, people will come to know about your product.

These are some of the ways through which you will be able to promote your product. But there are other ways. You need to price it very well and set up your shop where consumers will come and purchase it.

Resources

Important note: at the time of printing, all the websites listed in this book are correct and working OK. As the internet changes rapidly, some sites might no longer work when you read this book. This is, of course, out of our control.

Here are sites where you can find useful information about patents in the US and UK.

1. http://worldwide.escpacenet.com/advancedSearch
2. http://www.ipo.gov.uk/pro-types/pro-patent/pro-p-os/pr-p-find-number.htm
3. https://uk.practicallaw.thomsonreuters.com/2-504-4154?transitionType=Default&contextData=(sc.Default)&firstPage=true&bhcp=1
4. https://www.entrepreneur.com/article/83496
5. http://www.wipo.int/patents/en/topics/exceptions_limitations.html
6. https://en.wikipedia.org/wiki/Patent
7. http://ip.com/solutions/patent-validity/
8. https://www.alrc.gov.au/publications/9-challenging-and-enforcing-patent-rights/challenges-patent-rights
9. https://en.wikipedia.org/wiki/Patent_infringement
10. http://smallbusiness.findlaw.com/intellectual-property/patent-infringement-and-litigation.html
11. https://smallbiztrends.com/2018/05/patenting-an-idea.html
12. https://www.legislation.gov.uk/ukpga/1977/37
13. http://www.howdesign.com/design-creativity/how-to/how-to-sell-an-idea/
14. https://www.uspto.gov/
15. https://www.bl.uk/business-and-ip-centre/articles/whats-the-difference-between-unregistered-design-right-and-design-registration

16. https://www.gov.uk/guidance/manual-of-patent-practice-mopp/section-36-co-ownership-of-patents-and-applications-for-patents
17. https://www.gov.uk/browse/business/intellectual-property
18. https://www.uspto.gov/
19. https://www.gov.uk/design-right
20. https://www.gov.uk/guidance/plant-breeders-rights
21. http://www.brockwood-services.com/The_Nature_of_Patent_Rights.html
22. https://mbmcommercial.co.uk/jointly-owned-intellectual-property-how-to-live-in-e2-80-9charmony-e2-80-9d.html

Made in the USA
Columbia, SC
17 December 2024

49554644R00065